639.92 Ben
Bender, Kelly Conrad
Texas wildscapes :
    gardening for wildlife
CY $24.95
          ocn313017375
1st ed., Texas   11/09/2009

___ cassettes
_1_ discs/disks
___ videos
_1_ bks/pamphs

D1283958

Texas Wildscapes

GARDENING FOR WILDLIFE

The Texas A&M Nature Guides Edition

KELLY CONRAD BENDER

with contributions by

Noreen Damude, Diana Foss, Chris Lintz

& Elena Cano Camarillo

TEXAS A&M UNIVERSITY PRESS   COLLEGE STATION

This paper meets the requirements
of ANSI/NISO Z39.48-1992
(Permanence of Paper).
Binding materials have been
chosen for durability.

*Funding from the
Texas Parks and Wildlife Department
helped make this book possible.*

Library of Congress Cataloging-in-Publication Data

Bender, Kelly Conrad.
    Texas wildscapes : gardening for wildlife : the Texas A&M
nature guides edition / Kelly Conrad Bender. — 1st ed.
        p. cm.
    Includes bibliographical references.
    ISBN-13: 978-1-60344-085-1 (flexbound with flaps :
alk. paper)
    ISBN-10: 1-60344-085-2 (flexbound with flaps : alk.
paper)
1. Gardening to attract wildlife—Texas.
2. Natural landscaping—Texas.
3. Native plant gardening—Texas.   I. Title.
QL59.B456   2009
639.9'209764—dc22
2009007468

Illustrations, pages xiii, 47, 95 by Rob Fleming

Other illustrations by Jeremy George Boehm

Cover photograph and frontispiece © Micheline Young. Landscape design by Cathy Nordstrom,

San Souci Gardens. Pool and pergola designed, engineered, and constructed by Ed Young.

Contents

Preface to the Texas A&M Nature Guides Edition

In 1994, the Texas Parks and Wildlife Department made an important commitment to the urban and suburban areas of Texas by initiating the Texas Wildscapes Backyard Wildlife Habitat Program™. With the program, we aimed to educate residents and enrich their lives while enhancing wildlife habitat regardless of its proximity to people.

Since its introduction, Texas Wildscapes™ has evolved from simple information pamphlets packaged in a paperboard folder, to two editions of a full-color and information-packed book, and now to its latest incarnation as a book accompanied by a fully searchable, customizable, and updatable electronic product. Through the program, we have helped Texans improve 153,116 acres of wildlife habitat, touched tens of thousands of residents through our educational materials, programs, and workshops, and recognized more than 2,000 officially certified Texas Wildscapes™ and Best of Texas Backyard Habitat™ properties.

We recognize that 80 percent of Texans live in urbanized areas. We also understand that more than 95 percent of Texas land is privately owned. Urbanization continues to expand, eating up hundreds of acres of valuable habitat. But, as urbanization continues, we can still support valuable habitat by maintaining wildlife corridors with urban natural areas, engaging in conservation design, and maintaining and restoring natural waterways. Real habitat conservation in Texas can be achieved if we all work together in a close partnership that benefits the people of this state, our natural resources, and the fish and wildlife that we value so highly.

Whether you are providing habitat on a second-story apartment balcony or a 10,000-acre West Texas ranch, or are just becoming more educated about wildlife habitat and conservation techniques, we hope this Texas Wildscapes™ program provides you with the information you need to support a great conservation effort throughout Texas.

If this is your first exploration of wildlife habitat gardening, we welcome you to an exciting journey of discovering and supporting nature only steps from your back door. If you are expanding your knowledge of wildlife habitat through the Texas Wildscapes™ program, we hope you will find exciting and new information to help you better provide food, water, shelter, space, and native plants for wildlife. Regardless, we know you will enjoy the new and updated information included in *Texas Wildscapes: Gardening for Wildlife, the Texas A&M Nature Guides Edition,* and we look forward to our continued partnership with you to create a more habitat-rich Texas.

Naturally,
Kelly Conrad Bender
Texas Parks and Wildlife Department

Preface to the First Edition

The Texas Wildscapes Backyard Wildlife Habitat Program™ was developed by the Nongame and Urban Program (now the Wildlife Diversity Program) of Texas Parks and Wildlife in 1994. A major goal of the program is to create a greater amount of good wildlife habitat in urban and suburban areas by providing the public with the tools necessary to understand and appreciate the kinds of wildlife they can attract to their own backyards. Texas Wildscapes™ works by incorporating three key components necessary to support wildlife: food, water, and shelter. In addition, the program requires the use of at least 50 percent native Texas plants to provide good wildlife habitat in a landscape.

While your Wildscapes habitat might only support a few different species, whole neighborhoods full of Wildscape habitats will create a tapestry of habitat suitable to sustain wildlife. By creating and linking habitats to form a "patchwork quilt" of Wildscape habitats, a much larger area for wildlife can be provided.

When we watch nature programs on television, we may cheer as the nearly starving cheetah overtakes the gazelle, and watch with sad satisfaction as the cheetah then feeds the animal to her cubs. This, we reason, is nature. But nature does not cease when native animals enter our backyard sanctuaries. Caterpillars need to eat leaves in order to become butterflies, mammals need to raise their young, and hawks need to capture their bird and small mammal prey. All these animals are simply doing the things they need to do in order to survive and reproduce, just as we do. A caterpillar isn't "bad" because it eats the parsley plant, the snake isn't "bad" because it eats the eggs in a bird's nest, and humans aren't "bad" because we eat the eggs of a chicken and, to add insult to injury, the chicken too! When providing habitat for wildlife, we must keep an "ecosystem" frame of mind, realizing that animals simply do what they do, with neither valor nor malice, in order to survive and reproduce. When animals visit Wildscapes, whether for short periods to feed and bathe, or for longer periods to reside and nest, we can be assured that their habitat is complete.

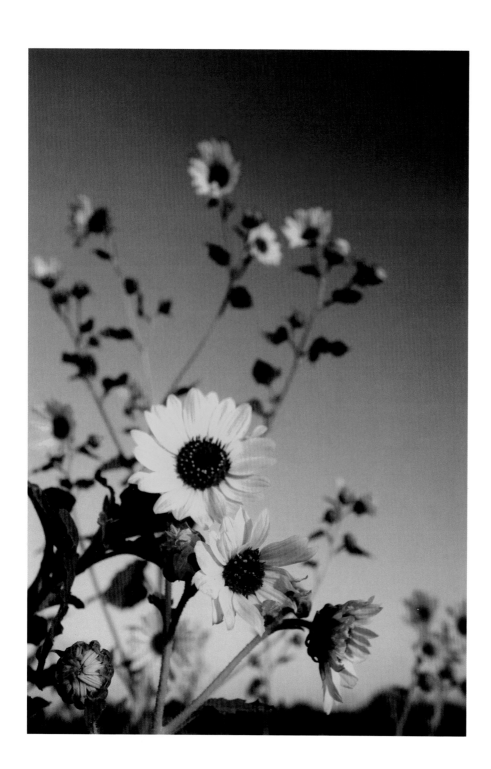

Acknowledgments

In the early years, the Texas Wildscapes™ program was supported by the tireless efforts of Noreen Damude, formerly of the Texas Parks and Wildlife Department (TPWD). Her oft-cited encyclopedic knowledge of the natural world, along with her talent for eloquent prose, allowed for the creation of an exceptional and nationally recognized program and established a foundation for its continued success. John Herron (formerly of TPWD) and Matt Wagner (TPWD) also enabled the success of the program by ensuring funding, department support, and adequate resources. Throughout the history of the program, its successive coordinators ensured it ran smoothly by promoting native wildlife habitat landscaping throughout the state, developing new and exciting educational materials and opportunities, and running the tedious but important administrative tasks required to keep the program going. These long-suffering champions include Noreen Damude, Elena Cano-Camarillo, and Mark Klym.

For the message of habitat conservation and restoration to reach an increasing number of urban and suburban Texans, the Texas Parks and Wildlife Department wisely developed the Urban Wildlife program, supported by talented and enthusiastic wildlife biologists willing to tackle the urban jungle. These biologists have included Lois Balin, Stephen Benn, Keith Crenshaw, John Davis, Diana Foss, Jesus Franco, Judit Gowen, Richard Heilbrun, Brett Johnson, Chuck Kowaleski, Rufus Stephens, Lou Verner, Ray Whitney, myself, and others.

The Texas Wildscapes™ program was designed and customized to fit the needs and strengths of Texas' natural resources, citizens, and government institutions. However, we are quick to recognize that the model provided by the National Wildlife Federation's Backyard Habitat Program™ was instrumental in developing our program. Additionally, we are proud to team with the National Wildlife Federation (NWF) in the Best of Texas Backyard Habitat Program™, a partnership supported by Alice Nance and Marya Fowler of NWF.

On a personal note, I am deeply grateful to my family for their support throughout my professional career. My husband, Steven, children, Noah and Will, parents, Marvin and Terry Conrad, and in-laws, Cliff and Donna Bender, were instrumental in inspiring and enabling me to pursue natural resource conservation as a career. Thank you.

Part 1
Welcome to Wildscaping!

CHAPTER ONE   *Creating a Wildscape*

We often imagine wildlife as exotic creatures from faraway lands. After all, what could be more exciting than African lions, polar bears, and birds of paradise? Those of us who live in urban and suburban areas may even forget that our very own Texas has any wildlife at all. Where we now have tracts of single family dwellings, sprawling malls, and concrete parking lots, wildlife such as kit foxes, meadowlarks, whiptail lizards, and bobcats once roamed. Where we now have seas of St. Augustine, pansies, and begonias, there were once waves of Indiangrass, Gulf Coast muhly, purple asters, butterfly-weed, and winecups. Texas Wildscapes™ is a program that can help us restore our lands for these native plants and animals. By creating a Wildscape, we can produce a well-balanced habitat which invites native wildlife into our own backyards.

Why Wildscaping Is Necessary

Texas is blessed with nearly 170 million acres of mostly rural countryside from the Chihuahuan Desert to pine forests. As a public land steward, the Texas Parks and Wildlife Department has been engaged in habitat restoration on wildlife management areas, state parks, and state natural areas totaling over one million acres. The remaining land, over 97% of the total acreage, is managed by private landowners. In order to sustain habitat for all species, we must also address areas of land held by the private landowners. Private land stewardship ensures the perpetuation of wildlife habitat through sustainable agricultural and wildlife management practices.

Changes in wildlife populations today are a reflection of progressive alteration and loss of habitat over time. As grasslands are converted to shrub lands and forests to pasture, wetlands are drained, and bottomland hardwoods are lost, dramatic changes in wildlife populations have also occurred. The physical structure of a habitat reflects the function of that habitat and the types of species that will find a home there. As a habitat changes, either due to natural factors such as flood or fire or by human actions, so will the wildlife populations that depend on that habitat.

Ecologists today frequently use the term "habitat fragmentation." Habitat fragmentation occurs where discontinuous land use creates irregular patches of habitats across the landscape, breaking up large blocks of pristine habitat such as forests, grasslands, and marshes. Today, habitat fragmentation is occurring rapidly in suburban fringe areas as development expands into former farm and ranch operations.

Establishing Wildscapes creates habitat for wildlife. This spider on a Maximilian sunflower is part of a healthy ecosystem.

Large land holdings are being increasingly subdivided. Roads, boundary fences, and utility easements are being constructed. If habitats become fragmented enough, the survival of many organisms will be threatened. Many exotic plants initially intended for backyard landscapes can also escape into the wild. Chinese tallow, once thought of as a harmless and beautiful landscape plant and valuable agricultural producer, has now replaced tens of thousands of acres of native vegetation, devastating plant and animal communities. Introduced insects such as the red imported fire ant have altered entire ecosystems by preying on native insects, as well as the eggs and young of small reptiles, birds, and mammals.

More than three quarters of the population of Texas is located in six cities: Austin, Dallas, El Paso, Fort Worth, Houston, and San Antonio. As these urban areas have grown, the land has changed from forests, prairies, and agricultural areas to suburban development. This transformation has resulted in extensive habitat fragmentation, creating land that is rendered nearly unusable to native wildlife because of the lack of connecting corridors. As Texas' human population continues to soar, more and more space is consumed to suit our needs. As a consequence, wildlife has been progressively squeezed out of the habitat it needs to survive. Happily, private residences and other developed properties hold a great potential for restoring quality, quantity, and richness of the wildlife habitat that has been displaced. Wildscapes can provide the bridges, corridors, and buffers to link privately owned lands to natural areas, parks, and green belts. Wildscaping translates into a total increase in healthy wildlife habitat and natural beauty.

Urban development is one major cause of habitat loss.

© TPWD

Benefits of Wildscaping

There are educational, environmental, economic, and aesthetic benefits to creating backyard habitat to attract wildlife. To realize the educational benefits of Wildscapes, simply observe young children encountering nature in the backyard for the first time. A wildlife garden can become the setting for learning about the life histories of birds, small mammals, insects, plants, and other creatures. By observing first-hand migration, hibernation, reproduction, and predation, children will likely learn more about the workings of nature than they could glean from books. By discovering the intricate balances in the natural world, Texans of all ages become better able to make informed decisions concerning the future of our community and the world. We can better understand important local environmental issues and how they impact our lives.

By maintaining a healthy wildlife habitat, we create healthier living for people. Plants in richly vegetated open spaces in urban and suburban areas absorb carbon dioxide and give off oxygen, thus renewing our air supply. Plant foliage captures dust and other pollutants, thus purifying the air we breathe. Vegetated areas aid in erosion control and the conservation of soils. Plant roots hold soils in place while plant parts above ground impede water runoff. A diverse landscape containing many species of native plants not only supports an abundance of wildlife, it also is less prone to large-scale devastation from

insect pests or diseases. Planting coniferous and deciduous trees, shrubs, and especially native grasses is an excellent erosion control measure, while also providing much needed cover and nesting sites for resident birds.

The economic benefits of creating a backyard habitat are also significant. Maintaining expansive manicured lawns, clipped hedges, and water-guzzling exotic plants can be many times more expensive than caring for native vegetation. Once established, native plant species require only minimal attention from the home gardener. This translates into a reduction of extensive soil amendments, less watering, and a reduced need for chemical pest control, chemical fertilizers, and pampering. Not only that, properly placed trees and shrubs can save home heating and cooling costs. Planted on the west or southwest side of a home, large deciduous shade trees will shelter the home from the onslaught of the hot summer sun. In the winter, the trees lose their leaves and allow the sun's rays to warm the house. Finally, planting or preserving vegetated slopes with cover for wildlife will also slow water and wind movement, decrease soil erosion, help replenish ground water reserves, reduce runoff, and decrease stream flow fluctuation. Conserving soils and safeguarding water quality improves overall ecosystem stability and saves money in the long run.

One has only to watch hummingbirds flying anxiously from flower to flower, chickadees and titmice snatching seeds from a feeder, or dazzling butterflies tilting lazily from blossom to blossom to understand that wildlife habitat is not only functional, but also aesthetically pleasing. People yearn to get back to nature. They have a compelling need for contact with the natural world.

A Wildscape gives us a sense of place, keeps us in touch with the passing seasons, and affords an avenue of escape from the chaos of everyday life.

The Trouble with Lawns

To observe the wonders of wildlife, we need to entice their presence. Unfortunately, expansive, well-manicured yards with clipped turf and only tall trees do not support a great diversity of wildlife. Despite the allure of a rich carpet of plushness under your feet, the truth is that a neatly manicured lawn extending from property line to property line will be nearly as devoid of wildlife as a parking lot. Unfortunately, the only species that particularly benefit from oceans of closely cropped turf are those "weedy," undesirable species such as grackles, starlings, and house sparrows. The greater the habitat diversity your property provides, the more types of wildlife will choose to visit your yard. A primary method to increase habitat diversity is to replace expansive lawns with a selection of native flowers, shrubs, and trees in a well thought-out arrangement.

A multilayered landscape containing many species of native plants not only supports an abundance of wildlife, it also provides insurance against the depredation of insect pests. Landscapes that contain a single species (monocultures) are impoverished systems and are highly vulnerable to diseases which can sweep in and wipe out everything.

Planting a variety of coniferous and deciduous trees, shrubs, and especially native grasses is an excellent way to diversify your habitat. It will also provide much needed cover and nesting sites to resident birds and other wildlife. Flowering plants in the legume family (those plants which produce a dry fruit, such as bean plants) provide nectar for bees and butterflies, while grasses offer larval food sources to several species of butterflies, particularly skippers. Both legumes and grasses also protect soils from erosion and excessive leaching.

Another good reason for growing less lawn is that

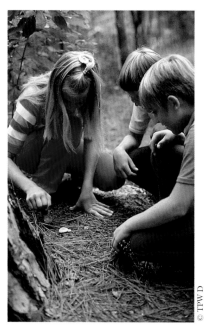

Natural habitats can be outdoor learning labs for children of all ages.

fertilizers and lawn chemicals invariably make their way into ponds and streams. Excess fertilizers foul our waters by increasing nutrient levels and encouraging heavy algal blooms. Finally, watering lawns accounts for 40–60% of residential water consumption, making lawn maintenance not only a chore but also a drain on the pocketbook and the water supply.

Consider reducing the size of your lawn areas and replacing them with natural ground covers, native grasses, trees, shrubs, vines, and wildflowers. If you desire to have areas of turf grass, try grasses that are appropriate for your soil and climate. Buffalograss *(Buchloe dactyloides)*, for example, is an excellent choice. It is native to many areas of Texas and is quite drought-tolerant. Mow any turf at a higher blade setting (no shorter than three inches) to reduce water use, and resist the urge to bag the clippings. Allow the clippings to remain in the turf to return nutrients to the soils. Less lawn means less water and chemical application, and less mowing. Who can argue with that?

For more information on caring for lawns, see *A Green Guide to Yard Care*, an informative brochure produced by the Texas Commission on Environmental Quality, and the "Don't Bag It" leaf management program sponsored by the AgriLife Extension (Texas A&M System).

Male great-tailed grackles display to each other in one of their favorite habitats: a well manicured lawn.

Texas Wildscapes Backyard Habitat Certification Program

As you watch your Wildscape habitat develop, let the world (or at least your neighborhood) know about your efforts. The Texas Parks and Wildlife Department is awarding official Texas Wildscape™ certifications to sites that fulfill the minimum requirements of providing food, water, and shelter to wildlife. Simply fill out the Texas Wildscapes Certification Application explaining how you provided habitat for wildlife and return it to Texas Parks and Wildlife. Once your application is approved, you will receive a personalized certificate and weather-resistant backyard sign that identifies your property as an officially certified Texas Wildscape™. To obtain an official Texas Wildscapes Certification Application by mail, send a request to:

Texas Wildscapes
4200 Smith School Road
Austin, Tx 78744

Or, download an application at:
www.tpwd.state.tx.us

Related Texas Parks and Wildlife Department Programs

The Texas Parks and Wildlife Department has introduced several programs which benefit Texas wildlife, wildlife habitat, and you. The goal of these programs is to help Texans become more involved in Texas wildlife. Many of these programs go hand-in-hand with Wildscaping, and you may wish to integrate these programs into your Wildscaping project.

For general information on Texas wildlife or park information, call 800-792-1112. For more information about wildlife in Texas, call the Wildlife Information Line at 512-389-4505. To receive a subscription to the Wildlife Diversity Program newsletter, *Eye on Nature*, contact the Wildlife Diversity Program at 512-389-4644. You can get answers to many wildlife questions by e-mailing nature@tpwd.state.tx.us.

Best of Texas Backyard Wildlife Habitat

The Best of Texas Backyard Habitat™ program is a joint effort of the National Wildlife Federation and Texas Parks and Wildlife Department that takes the best of our individual programs and pushes the bar a little higher, challenging Texas wildlife gardeners to create a habitat that seeks to maximize wildlife benefits and highlight sound conservation stewardship within the bounds of urban restrictions. Does your garden meet the challenge? If so, this may be just the program for you!

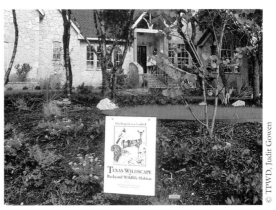

Once you have created a Wildscape, consider certifying it with Texas Parks and Wildlife.

To become certified as a Best of Texas Backyard Habitat™, complete the application (found in the "Wildlife" section of the Texas Parks and Wildlife Department Web site at www.tpwd.state.tx.us) and mail it with the certification fee ($30) to:

Best of Texas Backyard Habitats
National Wildlife Federation
Gulf States Natural Resource Center
44 East Avenue Suite 200
Austin, TX 78701

TEXAS HUMMINGBIRD ROUNDUP SURVEY
Join over 3500 other Texans to help us determine more about the range, distribution, favored sites, and feeding habits of Texas hummingbirds. When you join the survey, you help us learn more about these fascinating creatures by recording events that take place at your hummingbird feeder, such as which species you see, what flowers they prefer, and when each species arrives and departs for the season. The survey packet contains a survey form, information about Texas hummingbirds, a packet of native seeds for your hummingbird garden, and a hummingbird distribution map.

You can read about the results in the annual newsletter, and you will receive a colorful Hummingbird Roundup decal. The Hummingbird Wheel is a full-color hummingbird identification device that includes illustrations of all 18 Texas hummers, identification characteristics, and fun hummingbird facts, and is also available through the Wildlife Diversity Program for $11.95.

For more information, contact:
Texas Hummingbird Roundup Coordinator
Wildlife Diversity Wildlife Program
512-389-4644; nature@tpwd.state.tx.us
or:
Texas Hummingbird Roundup
4200 Smith School Road
Austin, Tx 78744

TEXAS PARTNERS IN FLIGHT
Texas Partners in Flight (PIF) is a nonprofit partnership of state and federal government agencies, non-government organizations, industries, communities, landowners, and individuals, and operates solely from the volunteer efforts and contributions of its partners to ensure healthy populations of Texas' magnificent bird resources.

For more information, contact:
State Coordinator of Texas
Partners in Flight at
nature@tpwd.state.tx.us
or:
Partners in Flight
506 Hayter St.
Nacogdoches, Tx 75965

TEXAS MASTER NATURALISTS
The Texas Master Naturalist™ program provides a place for all those Texans who long to get their hands dirty while helping themselves and others reconnect with the natural Texas. Master Naturalist™ students receive forty hours of locally relevant instruction and field experience and are asked to provide forty hours of nature-related volunteer service and obtain eight hours of advanced training each year to remain certified. Individual chapter registration fees and class times vary. With nearly forty chapters across the state, chances are good that there is already a fun, dedicated group of people meeting and working for conservation close by. For more information, see the Master Naturalist Web site (http://masternaturalist.tamu.edu).

Biologist removing exotic water hyacinth from Sheldon Lake.

PROJECT WILD/AQUATIC WILD

Project WILD/Aquatic WILD is "Wildlife in Learning Design." This environmental and conservation education program for kindergarten through twelfth grade students emphasizes awareness, appreciation, and understanding of wildlife and natural resources.

For more information contact:
> Project WILD/ Aquatic WILD Office
> 512-389-4369 or 800-792-1112

or:
> Project WILD/ Aquatic WILD
> Texas Parks and Wildlife
> 4200 Smith School Road
> Austin, Tx 78744

PRIVATE LANDS ENHANCEMENT PROGRAM

The goal of the Private Lands Enhancement Program is to provide expertise to land managers in the preservation and development of wildlife habitat and the proper management of the wildlife populations which utilize that habitat. Along with superb technical guidance, the program also offers the recent publication "Wildlife Management Associations and Co-ops."

For more information, contact:
> Program Director of Private Lands Enhancement
> Texas Parks and Wildlife
> 800-792-1112

or:
> Private Lands Enhancement
> 4200 Smith School Road
> Austin, Tx 78744

LONE STAR LAND STEWARD

Texas Parks and Wildlife sponsors the Lone Star Land Steward Award Program to recognize private landowners for excellence in habitat management and wildlife conservation on their lands. Ranchers, farmers, foresters, and other land managers and cooperatives may participate in this statewide awards program.

To receive a nomination form contact:
> Texas Parks and Wildlife
> Private Lands Enhancement Program
> 4200 Smith School Road
> Austin, Tx 78744

One of the goals of a Wildscape is to provide food and shelter for native wildlife with the use of native plants. As you plan your wildlife habitat, keep in mind that Texas is blessed with ten very different ecological regions (also known as ecoregions). An ecoregion is any geographical area that encompasses a distinct grouping of plant, animal, geological, and environmental features.

Gulf Coast seaoats.

ing regional descriptions. Check your soils first to determine if they contain clays, gumbos, or sands. (For more information on soils and soil types, see chapter four.) Remember that in suburban developments, builders have often scraped the topsoil away and replaced it with soil from other areas. To find out what kind of soil is naturally found in your area, examine soils in greenbelt areas, along railroad tracks, creeks, and other undeveloped areas. These locations can give you a pretty good indication of the natural soils and dominant native vegetation of your area. You may already have wonderful native species of trees, shrubs, and grasses growing on your property. These should be left in place. Your local native plant nursery person and soil conservation agent (Texas Natural Resources Conservation Service) can also provide useful information for your particular area.

When comparing two very different ecoregions such as the Trans-Pecos region of West Texas to the East Texas Pineywoods, it is easy to see the vast differences in Texas' landscapes. The Trans-Pecos is generally characterized as an area of low rainfall, high elevation, and sparse vegetation, while the East Texas Pineywoods is characterized by high rainfall, low elevation, complex soils, and lush vegetation. The animal and plant life adapted to each of these regions are completely different from one another as well. Therefore, a person in the western portion of the state would not want to create a habitat based on the wildlife and plant species of East Texas, nor would a person in East Texas be able to easily establish a Wildscape based on the vegetation of West Texas.

Because most of Texas' major cities are situated in areas where different soil and vegetational regions meet, it is sometimes not easy to know in which ecoregion you are located. Many metropolitan areas like San Antonio, Houston, Austin, and the Dallas–Fort Worth metroplex, for example, have two or three ecoregions. To know in which ecoregion you reside, first consult the Texas ecoregion map (figure 2a), then simply step outside your front door and take a look around. Compare your area with the follow-

FIGURE 2A

Ecological Regions of Texas

1 Pineywoods
2 Gulf Coast Prairies and Marshes
3 Post Oak Savannah
4 Blackland Prairies
5 Cross Timbers and Prairies
6 South Texas Plains
7 Edwards Plateau
8 Rolling Plains
9 High Plains
10 Trans-Pecos

The Ten Ecoregions of Texas

REGION ONE—PINEYWOODS

Mostly deep, dark, and evergreen, the Pineywoods region of East Texas is an extension of the rich pine/hardwood forests of the southeastern United States. Gently rolling hills cloaked with pines and oaks and rich bottomlands with tall hardwoods characterize these forests, while intermittent pockets of evergreen shrub bogs, open seepage slopes, and cypress-tupelo swamps form a patchwork quilt throughout. Frequent long-term flooding plays an essential role in maintaining these bottomland hardwood communities. The region's plants are adapted to the characteristic ridge and swale formations in the bottomland caused by periodic and often severe flooding. Eliminating the flooding alters the plant and animal life that have formed a unique and diverse community in the area.

Flowering dogwood trees, with their beautiful white bracts gleaming through the oak woodlands in the spring, are scattered about the moist uplands. The region's thirty-five to sixty inches of rain each year support not only pines, including loblolly, shortleaf, and longleaf pines, but swamp and streamside stands of hardwoods including beech, oaks, elm, and magnolia. In addition, the Pineywoods host a myriad of woodland specialties such as sphagnum mosses, ferns, pitcher plants, sundews, pipeworts, and orchids.

Elevations range from near sea level to almost 500 feet with an average annual temperature of 66° F. The growing season ranges from 250 days in the southern portion of the region to 230 days near the Red River in the north. Highly weathered soils are sandy or loamy and very deep. Most of the 15.8 million acres of the region is prime timber land, and conversion of these woodlands to plantations of loblolly or slash pine has drastically altered many of the natural forest communities.

East Texas boasts a rich diversity of wildlife. Fifteen species of Texas breeding birds nest predominantly in this ecoregion. Three of these species—the pine warbler, brown-headed nuthatch, and the endangered red-cockaded woodpecker—are confined almost exclusively, in Texas, to the Pineywoods forest for breeding. The Bachman's sparrow nests locally in Texas only in the longleaf pine uplands of this region, while wintering and nesting bald eagles set up roosts or nest sites in undisturbed woodlands near rivers and lakes. Other avian specialties of the Pineywoods include the wood thrush, hooded warbler, prothonotary warbler, and barred owl, the dark-eyed, noisy denizen of deep bottomland forests. Characteristic mammals of the region include the river otter, gray squirrel, flying squirrel, and possibly the Louisiana black bear. Although the Louisiana black bear is currently absent from the Pineywoods, suitable habitat still exists to support future populations of this East Texas specialty.

Pineywoods.

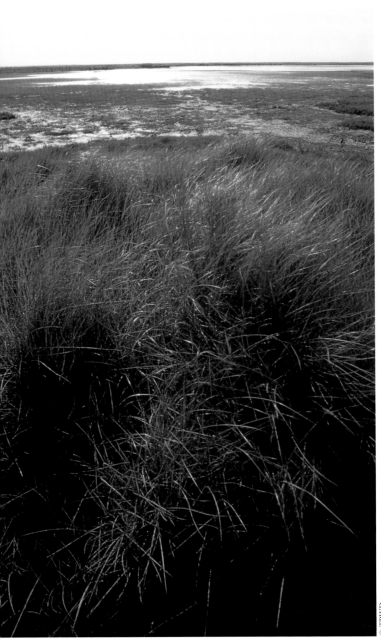

Gulf Coast Prairies and Marshes.

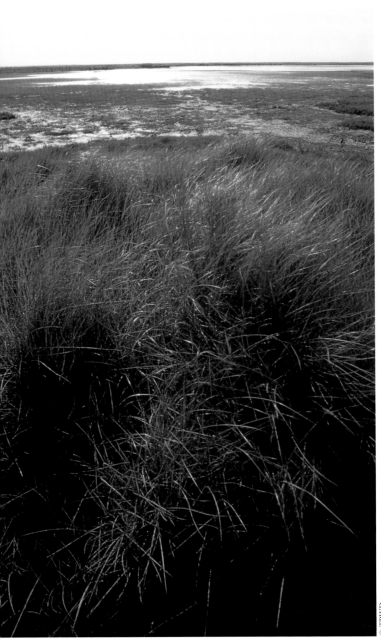 © TPWD

tain more clay than the marsh areas and are very rich in nutrients. The character of the coastline is shaped by the long and continuous confrontation with the sea, wind, and rain. Storms shape the shoreline as a sculptor works clay, creating shallow bays, estuaries, salt marshes, dunes, and tidal flats. Because of the proximity to the Gulf of Mexico, many plants are halophytic, or highly salt tolerant.

The Coastal Bend begins at midcoast near Corpus Christi where the shoreline is edged by Mustang and Padre Islands, part of the longest chain of barrier islands in the world. Here, island dunes are dappled with seaoats, glasswort, beach evening-primrose, and railroad vine—hardy colonizers of the shifting beachhead sands. Sandy soils of the Coastal Bend also support distinctive chenier woodlands of scrub oaks, yaupon, red-bay, and wax-myrtle. Tallgrass and midgrass prairies, as well as Spartina grass marshes, make up a major portion of the coastal vegetation. Tallgrass prairies extending from the Great Plains to the Midwest are characterized by taller grasses, deeper soils, and more precipitation than short- or midgrass prairies farther west.

Much of the upland areas are dissected with numerous sluggish rivers, bayous, creeks, and sloughs. Between the rivers, little bluestem, Indiangrass, and various sedges dominate extensive open prairies. At one time, the coastal river bottoms of this area were clothed in woodlands of sugarberry, pecan, elm, and coastal live oak. Few such areas remain today, as most of these prairies are farmed or have been absorbed into urban areas. Much of the remaining native sod of the Coastal Prairies has been invaded by exotics such as Macartney rose and Chinese tallow or native woody species including mesquite, prickly-pear, acacias, and scrub oaks. Today cattle graze the Coastal Prairies, farmers use the rich soils to grow rice, corn, grain sorghum, and cotton, while the oil and petrochemical industries dominate the northeastern end of this region.

Coastal areas are very rich in wildlife. Where treeless earth meets endless sky, coastal marshes harbor hundreds of thousands of wintering geese and ducks and provide critical landfall in the spring for neotropical migratory birds. The area is home to several important wildlife sanctuaries and refuges—notably

REGION TWO—GULF COAST PRAIRIES AND MARSHES

The Gulf Coast Prairies and Marshes follow the lip of the Texas coast and extend inland about sixty miles. This 9.5 million-acre swath of land traces a broad arc along the coast from the Sabine River to Baffin Bay. Elevations range from near sea level to almost 150 feet, and annual temperatures range from 70° F to 74° F. Soils of the marshy areas include acid sands, sandy loams, and clay. Soils of the Gulf prairies conthose protecting the endangered Attwater's prairie-chicken and the whooping crane. In the fall, coastal dunes serve as sentry roosts for southward-bound migrating peregrine falcons, while at any season there are lone willets, mini-battalions of sanderlings, and congregations of gulls, terns, and black skimmers feeding or loafing near the surf.

REGION THREE—POST OAK SAVANNAH

Lying immediately west of the Pineywoods, the Post Oak Savannah emerges almost imperceptibly, marked by subtle changes in soils and vegetation. Occupying approximately 8.5 million acres, the area's topography is gently rolling to hilly with elevations ranging from 300 to 800 feet, rainfall averages from 35 to 45 inches per year from west to east, with annual average temperatures ranging from 65° F to 70° F. Soils of the Post Oak Savannah are interesting and complex. They are usually acidic, with sands and sandy loams occurring on the uplands, clay to clay loams on the bottomlands, with a dense clay pan underlying all soil types. Because of this peculiarity, the Post Oak Savannah is sometimes referred to as the "Clay Pan Savannah." Clay pan soils are nearly impervious to water and underlie the surface layers of soil at depths of only a few feet. As a consequence, the moisture available for plant growth is limited, making the habitat surprisingly arid at times. One curious exception to the clay pan soils occurs in Bastrop County—home of the renowned Lost Pines. The Carrizo sands, a sandy inclusion of moist soils, harbor a unique community of loblolly pine, post oak, and blackjack oak and is also home to sphagnum bogs with ferns and carnivorous pitcher plants.

The Post Oak Savannah is punctuated by scattered oaks—mainly post oaks, of course—and blackjack oaks. Black hickory may also be locally abundant. Widespread trees of lesser importance include cedar elm, sugarberry, eastern red cedar, and common persimmon. Other important species of the region are Southern red oak, sassafras, flowering dogwood, yaupon, and winged elm. Some authorities believe that this region was once predominantly a tallgrass prairie, but that trees (mostly oaks) and brushy shrubs proliferated with the suppression of fires and the conversion of the land to farming and grazing. When fires were frequent, the land was not as it appears today. Historically, wide vistas of tallgrasses—little bluestem, Indiangrass, switchgrass—and a myriad of wildflowers, broken only by the occasional motte of venerable "giants," lent a parklike atmosphere to the landscape. Peat bogs, like the ones found in the Pineywoods, are also found here, mingled amongst stands of flowering dogwood, sassafras, bumelia, and yaupon.

Early European settlers were especially attracted to the Post Oak Savannah because it was clearly transitional between woodland and prairies. Today, the Post Oak Savannah is used largely for improved pasture, with vast acreages seeded to introduced grasses such as Bahia grass or Bermuda grass.

Mostly prairie animals with some woodland species abound in the Post Oak Savannah region. The distinctive sandy inclusion of the Lost Pines area also harbors one of the last refuges for the endangered Houston toad.

Post Oak Savannah.

© TPWD, Jim Yantis

Blackland Prairies.

REGION FOUR—BLACKLAND PRAIRIES

Taking their name from the fertile, dark clay soil, the Blackland Prairies constitute a true prairie ecosystem and have some of the richest, naturally fertile soils in the world. Characterized by gently rolling to nearly level topography, the land is carved by rapid surface drainage. Pecan, cedar elm, various oaks, soapberry, honey locust, hackberry, and Osage orange dot the landscape, with some mesquite invading from the south. A true tallgrass prairie, the dominant grass is little bluestem. Other important grasses include big bluestem, Indiangrass, eastern gamagrass, switchgrass, and sideoats grama. Elevations from 300 to more than 800 feet match those of the Post Oak Savannah, the annual rainfall varies from thirty to forty inches west to east, and the average annual temperatures range from approximately 66° F to 70° F. Described as "black velvet" when freshly plowed and moistened from a good rain, true blackland soils are deep, dark, calcareous deposits renowned for their high productivity. Scientists believe the richness of the prairie soils is derived from the abundant invertebrate fauna and fungal flora found in the soils themselves. Like many of the prairie communities comprising the Great Plains of North America, the Blackland Prairies harbor few rare plants or animals. The Blackland Prairies are today almost entirely brought under the plow, with only 5,000 acres of the original 12 million remaining. For this reason, many authorities believe that the Blackland Prairies represent one of the rarest landscapes in Texas.

REGION FIVE—CROSS TIMBERS AND PRAIRIES

The Cross Timbers and Prairies region covers about 17 million acres of alternating bands of wooded habitat crossing throughout a mostly prairie region—thus the term Cross Timbers. Elevations range from about 600 to almost 1,700 feet while rainfall varies from about twenty-five inches in the west and thirty-five inches in the east. Average annual temperatures are about 67° F. The Cross Timbers share many of the same species with the Post Oak Savannah. Grassland species such as little bluestem, Indiangrass, and big bluestem are common to both, but there are a few notable differences in floral composition. Yaupon, sassafras, and dogwood which form dense understory thickets in the Post Oak Savannah are almost nonexistent in the Eastern Cross Timbers. Texas mulberry, American elm, and Osage orange become more common. In the understory are rusty blackhaw viburnum, American beautyberry, Arkansas yucca, and smooth sumac. In the Western Cross Timbers, which is drier still, live oak becomes more important, replacing the post oaks as you proceed westward. The decrease in moisture discourages trees from growing close together except along streams, resulting in more expansive pockets of prairies separating isolated stands of trees. Here flameleaf sumac, redbud, Mexican plum, rusty blackhaw viburnum, and eastern red cedar are more prevalent. Fragrant sumac appears for the first time, a common shrub in the Western Cross Timbers, the Edwards Plateau, and further west. Wildlife consists of a mixture of eastern forest and prairie species.

REGION SIX—SOUTH TEXAS PLAINS

Bounded on the west by the Rio Grande and Mexico and on the north by the Balcones Escarpment, the South Texas Plains are vast, serene, and lightly populated. Elevations range from sea level to 1,000 feet and rainfall varies from 30 inches in the east to 16 inches in the west. Soils are varied and highly complex. Generally extremely basic to slightly acidic, they range from deep sands to tight clays and clay loams. With average annual temperatures around 73° F, the South Texas Plains boasts the longest growing season in Texas, lasting up to 365 days in some years at Brownsville. This warm region is, however, a land of recurrent droughts, a factor which distinctly marks the landscape. Nearly everything that grows here is drought-tolerant since rainfall is well below the amount needed for conventional forest trees. Sporadic rains, however, will trigger wildflowers to bloom unexpectedly at almost any time of year.

Cross Timbers and Prairies.

The South Texas region owes its diversity to the convergence of the Chihuahuan desert to the west, the Tamaulipan thornscrub and subtropical woodlands along the Rio Grande to the south, and the coastal grasslands to the east. Essentially a gently rolling plain, the region is cut by arroyos and streams and is blanketed with low growing vegetation—mesquite, granjeno, huisache, catclaw, blackbrush, cenizo, and guayacan. Wherever conditions are suitable, there is a dense understory of smaller trees and shrubs such as coyotillo, paloverde, Mexican olive, and various species of cacti. The woody vegetation of the South Texas Plains is so distinctive that the area is also referred to as the "brush country."

The Lower Rio Grande Valley is a highly distinctive subregion of the South Texas Plains. Usually defined as Cameron, Willacy, Hidalgo, and Starr counties, it contains the only subtropical area in Texas. Once supporting majestic groves of Sabal palms, Montezuma cypress, tall ebony-anaqua woodlands, and jungle-like expanses of Tamaulipan thorny shrubs, today much of it has been bulldozed, plowed, or paved. In fact, the once extensive groves of the native Sabal palm, which used to flourish here, are now reduced to only a few stands near Brownsville. Soils in this subtropical region range from sands to heavy clays. Clay soils and areas with extremely poor drainage dominate the resaca areas (old meandering paths of the Rio Grande).

Despite a history of land use which is the oldest in the state, the Rio Grande Plains harbor many rare species of plants and animals. It is here that a few wild tropical cats—ocelots and jaguarundis—still take refuge. Other special animals include ferruginous pygmy-owl, green jay, elf owl, Texas tortoise, indigo snake, and Mexican burrowing toad. There are also a surprising number of plants that occur here and nowhere else, especially among the cactus family, like Albert's black lace cactus, star cactus, and Runyon's cory cactus.

South Texas Plains.

Edwards Plateau.

REGION SEVEN—EDWARDS PLATEAU

Semi-arid, rocky, and beautifully rugged, the Edwards Plateau comprises nearly 24 million acres of land dominated by Ashe juniper, various oaks, and honey mesquite. Much of the region overlays a foundation of honey-combed Cretaceous limestone —and an immense underground reservoir called the Edwards Aquifer which spills out into many crystal clear springs. Caliche slopes, limestone escarpments, and thin clay soils are riddled with fossil remains of microscopic marine creatures, bearing testimony to the once massive sea that covered most of the state.

Topography is generally rough with elevations ranging from slightly less than 1,000 feet to over 3,000 feet and annual rainfall varies from a meager fifteen inches in the west to more than thirty-three inches in the east. Droughts can be prolonged, frequent, and often unpredictable. Sporadic flash floods can be devastating to those unaccustomed to their fury. Average temperatures range from 64° F to 67° F, and soils range from neutral to slightly acidic sands and sandy loams in the Llano Uplift, to thin, rocky, highly calcareous clays and clay loams over the rest of the Plateau.

It is a region of great floral diversity, with 100 of the 400 Texas endemic plants occurring only here, including Texas snowbells, bracted twist-flower, Texabama croton, Texas wildrice, and rock quillwort. Tucked away in protected valleys are relict populations of Texas madrone, Texas smoke tree, witch hazel, and big-tooth maple—trees normally found far to the northeast in Arkansas, to the west in the Trans-Pecos mountains, or to the south in the mountains of Mexico. The moist river corridors of the Colorado, Guadalupe, Blanco, and Nueces are lined with majestic bald cypress, pecan, hackberry, and sycamores. And perhaps nowhere else are the spring wildflowers so spectacular as in this region, with undulating tapestries of bluebonnets, Indian paintbrush, gaillardia,

Rolling Plains.

and golden-wave dazzling even the most jaded eye come April.

The region also hosts a number of terrestrial vertebrates. Here the white-tailed deer is king. Other common denizens of the Hill Country include armadillo, black-tailed jackrabbit, opossum, and Texas earless lizard. The purity and constant temperature of the waters provide ideal habitat for specialized spring dwellers such as the Clear Creek gambusia, the San Marcos gambusia, the fountain darter, and the San Marcos salamander. The unique Guadalupe bass and the Cagle's map turtle make their homes within the clear waters of the larger rivers. Thousands of caves of all sizes harbor cave shrimp and blind salamanders, which live only within the confines of these underground systems. Rare invertebrates like blind spiders, pseudoscorpions, mold beetles, and harvestmen are also found in caves, as well as Mexican free-tailed bats, which establish summer nursery colonies within several larger caves throughout the region.

The Edwards Plateau also provides a meeting ground for birds typical of both eastern and western regions. The green kingfisher, cave swallow, black-capped vireo, and golden-cheeked warbler nest more commonly here than in any other region in the state.

REGION EIGHT–ROLLING PLAINS

Marking the southern end of the Great Plains of the central United States, the red Rolling Plains represents the "last gasp" of a great continental prairie ecosystem. As its name suggests, topography of the Rolling Plains is gently rolling to moderately rough, with elevations ranging from 800 to 3,000 feet. Rainfall averages between thirty inches in the east to twenty-two inches in the west, the annual temperatures range from 60° F to 64° F. Most of the soils are neutral to slightly basic. The land is a varied and beautiful assortment of reds, from burnt sienna to the palest of pinks. East of the Caprock, on heavier clay soils, the native prairies of the Rolling Plains once consisted of midgrass and tallgrass communities nurtured by the intense summer rains and hot summer days. Pristine pockets of prairie are a rarity today, however. Much of what was once a sweeping expanse of sideoats grama, little bluestem, and blue grama has been tilled for grain fields or cotton. In many areas, overgrazing has allowed honey mesquite and shinnery oak to spread into the prairies, along with snakeweed and prickly-pear. Trees occurring along waterways and canyons of the Caprock include plains cottonwood, Mohr oak, netleaf hackberry, one-seed juniper, and Rocky Mountain juniper.

The gently rolling hills and broad flats of the Rolling Plains are the birthplace of many great Texas rivers, including the Canadian, the Colorado, the Concho, and the Red River, which originate in the brakes of the Caprock Escarpment and in the western reaches of the region. These rivers and their tributaries harbor their own unique inhabitants such as the Concho water snake and Brazos water snake which live only in a few restricted areas of the Colorado and Brazos river systems, respectively. Sand bars in the upper reaches of these rivers provide nesting habitat for the uncommon interior least tern and the snowy plover. Juniper woodlands, on the steep breaks of the canyons, are home to the Palo Duro mouse, a close relative of the pinyon mouse of the Rocky Mountains. Burrowing at the base of mesquite trees as they forage by night for seeds and greens, the Texas kangaroo rat is restricted to certain clay-loam soils of the Rolling Plains. This unique desert-adapted rodent still has scientists guessing as to its origins.

REGION NINE–HIGH PLAINS

Described as a sea of waving grasslands, the High Plains extends from the Panhandle south to the Pecos River. This 20 million-acre region fills most of the "handle" portion of the state and consists of a relatively high and level plateau of sandy to heavy dark, calcareous clay soils lying over an impervious layer of caliche. Soils consist mainly of outwash sediments from the Rocky Mountains. Elevations range from 3,000 to 4,700 feet, with an average annual temperature of approximately

High Plains

59° F. Winters here are the coldest in Texas. Rainfall averages from twenty-one inches on the eastern edge of the region to as low as twelve inches on the southwestern edge, and sun and wind rob the soil of what little moisture it receives.

Today an arid, treeless plain, much of the High Plains is irrigated from the vast Ogallala aquifer, the chief source of fresh water in the region. Classified as mixed-prairie and short-grass prairie, the vegetation varies as a function of location. Hardlands, mixed lands, sandy lands, draws, or caliche lakes give rise to distinct differences in plant communities. Though characteristically free from trees or brush, honey mesquite and yucca have invaded some areas, while sandsage and shinnery oak have spread through the sandylands. Playa lakes play an essential role in this region, as they are among the prime waterfowl wintering grounds for the North American Central Flyway. The region's other name, Llano Estacado or "Staked Plains" is thought to derive from the first European settlers to traverse the High Plains who drove stakes into the ground to help guide them across the flat, featureless plain. These early pioneers found a vast carpet of short grasses, home to enormous herds of buffalo and pronghorn antelope.

But what was new to early European pioneers was well known to numerous other groups who had inhabited the High Plains for over 12,000 years. Five hundred years ago, the region was settled by villages populated by the ancestors of Wichita or Pawnee bands. With the introduction of horses, sheep, and cattle to Spanish settlements in New Mexico, indigenous people were sequentially displaced by more recent emigrants representing the horse-riding nomadic people of the Apache, Comanche, and Kiowa nations.

While the plow and barbed wire fence have forever changed the original character of the High Plains, unique areas still remain, including scattered sand dunes cloaked with Havard shin-oak, sandsage, and little bluestem. Tallgrass meadows still wave in the breezes along the Canadian River and its tributaries, nourished by underground water flowing through the sands. While few rivers actually cross the High Plains, the thin ribbons of meager water along the Canadian and Red rivers once sustained luxuriant growths of tall willows and cottonwoods. Now two Old-World exotic plants, Russian olive and tamarisk,

have supplanted the native trees that line the banks, providing alternate homes for versatile phoebes and kingbirds. Grasses still provide cover and nesting habitat for myriads of other birds, and belts of trees planted back in the 1930s provide shelter to an amazing diversity of wildlife. Whereas gray wolves, grizzly bears, and elk no longer occur on the High Plains, mountain lions, the adaptable coyote, red-tailed hawk, and the diminutive swift fox now sit at the top of the food chain. And while the once vast populations of prairie dogs have dwindled, flocks of wintering waterfowl still frequent the ephemeral playa lakes, as do sandhill cranes and shorebirds which forage along the playa margins. Scattered bunches of lesser prairie-chickens still boom on the prairies, though their numbers are greatly reduced, while migrating flocks of lark buntings and horned larks still ply the skies over restless grassland seas.

REGION TEN—TRANS-PECOS

The Trans-Pecos is perhaps the most remarkable ecoregion of Texas, offering at once breathtakingly spectacular vistas and incredible biological diversity. Located west of the Pecos River are 19 million acres featuring an impressive array of habitats from desert grasslands, desert scrub, salt basins, sand hills, and rugged plateaus to wooded mountain slopes with summits that support mixed hardwood and coniferous forests. The Trans-Pecos as a whole represents the largest United States portion of true Chihuahuan Desert. This combination of Chihuahuan desert flats with more humid mountain ranges of diverse geological origin creates a living museum of biological wonders. More rare and endemic species are found among its desert valleys, grassy plateaus, wooded mountains, and protected canyons than in any other part of Texas. Indeed, one out of five Texas endemic plants occurs here and nowhere else.

Parts of this region are the hottest and driest in Texas with the western-most reaches receiving a scant eight inches of annual rainfall, sometimes even less. The average annual temperature of 64° F over the entire area does not reflect temperature extremes, heat being an important feature of the area. With elevations ranging from 2,500 feet to slightly over 8,500 feet, precipitation levels increase with increasing elevation giving rise to more moisture-loving communities in the mountainous areas. Soils are exceedingly com-

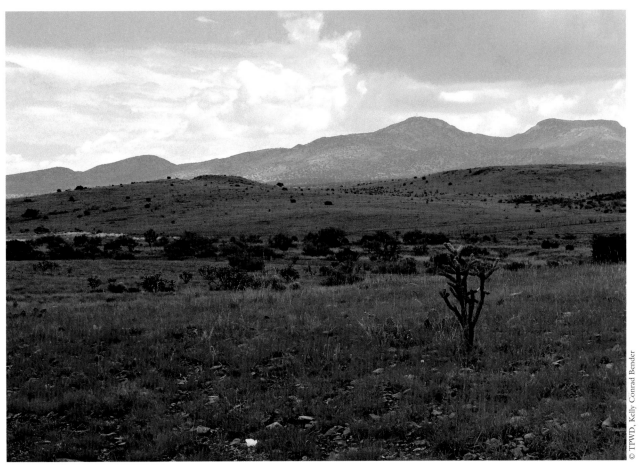

Trans-Pecos.

plex, ranging from very alkaline limestone-derived soils to highly acidic volcanically derived soils.

The Trans-Pecos cannot really be considered a single unit at all. For what occurs on the summit of the south rim of the Chisos Mountains—alligator juniper, Texas madrone, ponderosa pine, for example—bears no resemblance to the vegetation of the surrounding desert which includes creosote, tarbush, ocotillo, and lechuguilla. Generally, the land is dominated by creosote-tarbush desert-scrub grasslands with scattered inclusions of montane ponderosa pine, pinyon pine, and oak forests along with yucca and juniper savannahs, grama grasslands, and saltbush and alkali sacaton-dominated salt basins. Much of the landscape is dominated by desert grassland, but many of the desirable grasses have been replaced by lower quality plants due to continuous overgrazing. Stream courses, or riparian areas, are the oases of the desert, yet few remain relatively undisturbed. These areas support stands of willows, cottonwoods, sycamores, ash, and little walnuts. In these spring canyons, plants that cannot tolerate the rigors of dry desert conditions find refuge in the cool, moist surroundings.

A total of fifty-four species of birds are primarily confined to this region, among them the crissal thrasher, the black-tailed gnatcatcher, Gambel's quail, and Lucy's warbler. In fact, the Chisos Mountains is the only place in Texas where one can reliably find the Lucifer hummingbird, Mexican jay, Hutton's vireo, and painted redstart. Reptiles abound, notably the eastern collared lizard, southwestern blackneck garter snake, and the Trans-Pecos rat snake. Mammals are equally diverse with Mexican long-tongued bat, spotted bat, Texas antelope squirrel, kit fox, and bighorn sheep occurring mainly in this region. Black bears and mountain lions still inhabit the region, although the native populations of wapiti and grizzly bear are long gone. Finally, unique species of desert-adapted and relict pupfish, mosquito fish, and shiners make their homes in the few remaining undisturbed desert watercourses and cienegas.

Primary source: Texas Diversity: From the Pineywoods to the Trans-Pecos. In The Nature Conservancy News: 32 (5) by S. Winkler.

© John Herron

© TPWD

Step outside your back door and take a good look around. Perhaps you see a tree or two, a fence on your boundary line, maybe some clipped hedges, a few shrubs, and most probably a well-kept lawn over the vast majority of your backyard. Maybe there is a bird feeder hanging off a nearby tree limb. Overall, it is quite an attractive scene. However, your pretty backyard could be much more. It could be a haven for birds and other kinds of wildlife. Establishing a small wildlife sanctuary in your backyard will reward you by attracting a variety of animals for you to enjoy viewing. Many of these animals will visit, and some may actually stay to nest and rear their young in your backyard. The secret to attracting wildlife consists of supplying them with three basic requirements for survival: food, cover, and water.

By choosing your birdseed carefully, you can attract a wide variety of birds, such as these gregarious American goldfinches.

© John Herron

Food

Naturally occurring vegetation or native species of plants can provide food to wildlife species in your area. A variety of trees, shrubs, grasses, and flowers are good food sources, providing acorns, nuts, berries, buds, fruit, nectar, and seeds that can be used by a variety of wildlife. For a year-round supply of food, choose different plantings that produce food throughout each of the four seasons.

Deciduous plantings generally bear the most fruit, nuts, and seeds for wildlife. In addition, they offer shady, leafy nest sites. However, they shed their sheltering leaves in autumn. Evergreens, which bear leaves throughout the year, offer a good source of berries and seed-filled cones. They also offer year-round shelter, protection, and some breeding sites.

When vegetation cannot supply enough food for wildlife, you can supplement with feeders. There are three main types of feeders: hanging feeders, ground feeders, and suet feeders. Regardless of what type of feeder you choose, regular maintenance and cleaning is important to keep the feeder disease-free and to keep the seeds, nectar, or suet from spoiling. Usually, no more than a two-day supply of food should be placed in the feeders at a time.

HANGING FEEDERS

Hanging feeders are exactly that: feeders that hang from a tree limb or other overhead support. Fill them with either sugar water for nectarivores such as hummingbirds, orioles, and some bats, or seeds for seed-eating birds and mammals such as chickadees, titmice, and squirrels. When providing a seed feeder for birds, it may be best to use sunflower seeds only. Sunflower seeds are the number one choice of most seed-eating birds, especially the easy-to-shell and high-calorie black-oil sunflower seeds. If a feeder is filled with mixed seeds, wildlife will often toss aside unwanted seeds to get to their favorites. This practice can get expensive and create a mess under the feeder. Squirrels love sunflower seeds also, so you may have to protect your hanging feeder with a baffle—a dome-shaped cover placed above the feeder. This deters squirrels from jumping onto your feeder to eat the seeds and destroying your feeder. Place nectar feeders out for hummingbirds especially during the migration times of March through May, and August though early October. During these times you will be almost guaranteed to see a few of these flying jewels. To minimize fighting between the belligerent birds, space the feeders widely around your yard.

GROUND FEEDERS

Ground feeders vary from an elevated feeding tray placed on the ground and filled with seeds to simply tossing seeds directly on the ground. When used along with hanging feeders, a ground feeder will often distract squirrels from the other feeders. Cracked corn provides an inexpensive source of starch for large ground-feeding birds and squirrels. You can also supply the feeder with mixed seeds such as millet and peanut kernels, which will keep squirrels and most ground-feeding birds busy and happy.

SUET FEEDERS

A suet feeder dispenses suet (hard beef fat from the kidneys and loins) which is a good high energy food source during winter months. Many birds enjoy a suet feeder, and you will attract a variety of them to your feeder, especially woodpeckers such as the downy, ladder-backed, red-bellied, golden-fronted woodpeckers, and yellow-bellied sapsuckers.

To make this type of feeder, simply place hard fat in an old onion bag and hang it outside on a tree limb. Give birds a special treat by adding a variety of favorite seeds and raisins to the melted suet. For a decorative suet feeder, dip pine cones in the warm, melted fat mixture and allow it to cool and set. Vegetable shortening can also be used in place of beef fat. Suet feeders are ideal during cold weather, but suet becomes rancid very quickly during warm weather. In Texas, suet feeders should be watched closely for spoilage.

Cover

Wild animals are always on the alert for danger. Providing cover in your Wildscape will create wildlife refuges and safe havens for visitors. Understandably, wildlife that find shelter in your backyard habitat will feel safer and be more likely to eat, drink, and nest in your backyard habitat. By providing shelter, you can be assured that wildlife will find the one component that will most allow them to survive in your habitat: protection for themselves and their offspring from the weather and predators.

SHRUBS

You can provide a variety of structures and objects that are readily used by wildlife. A few well-placed brushy shrubs are the perfect hiding place for frightened animals such as birds, squirrels, or rabbits.

The dense growth will not only keep these small animals out of sight of predators, but it also provides protection from adverse weather conditions. Shrubs are also useful to birds such as cardinals, mockingbirds, and thrashers, since these birds use the thickly growing branches as nesting habitat. Planting thick evergreen shrubs, such as juniper and yaupon holly, will give wildlife shelter even in the winter, when other vegetation has shed its leaves. While shrubs provide a safer retreat from predators, they can also serve as a hiding place for predators as well. For this reason, shrubs should not be placed too close to areas where animals may be otherwise occupied, such as at bird baths, feeders, ponds, and nest boxes.

You can replace valuable shelter by constructing a brush pile, like this one, in locations such as along the edges of fields, forests, and wetlands.

Standing dead trees (snags) and fallen logs, like this one, are extremely valuable structures for wildlife.

BRUSH PILES

Another way to provide shelter for wildlife is to construct a brush pile by piling together loose brush, sticks, and small trees (such as old Christmas trees). Brush piles serve as a haven for small animals such as lizards, rabbits, woodrats, and even birds. The piles should be dense enough to protect wildlife from predators, cold wind, and rain, but loose enough to allow free passage into and out of the shelter. Some good locations for brush piles include forest edges and forest openings, field corners and edges, margins between streams and wetlands, near land that is being cleared, near forests that are being thinned, and along pond edges where the pile can be partially submerged. It is important to note that while brush piles are extremely valuable to wildlife, they may also attract household pests. For this reason, brush piles should not be located too close to your home.

SNAGS

Standing dead trees, called snags, provide for a great variety of wildlife. Woodpeckers excavate nesting cavities in soft, dead wood, and after the woodpeckers vacate their nests, other birds and mammals will enlarge the holes and nest there as well. Chickadees, nuthatches, titmice, bluebirds, some owls, wrens, tree swallows, raccoons, flying squirrels, and even some bats will nest or roost in these excavations. A few bats and the brown creeper, a tiny forest bird, will even roost under the loose bark of snags during the winter.

Originally, large hollow snags were the preferred nesting site of chimney swifts. Since much of this habitat has been cleared, they have adapted and moved to masonry chimneys which offer the same type of structure and are far more abundant than the hollow snags. Wide scale capping of residential chimneys on newer houses is reducing what was once a commonly available nest site.

Snags are also very attractive homes for insects, fungi, and microorganisms that help decompose the wood of the tree. Many of these species are eagerly hunted by various birds, reptiles, and mammals. Snags, therefore, not only provide roosting and nesting opportunities, but also provide a well-stocked "restaurant" for wildlife.

NEST BOXES

If there are no snags available on your property, you may want to construct a nest box to house one of the approximately fifty species of North American birds that are known to utilize bird houses for nesting. Most cavity-nesting birds are insectivorous and thus play an important part in the control of insect pests. Many small mammals also use nest boxes. To provide a nest box for the birds and mammals in your area, you must first decide which species you want to attract. Nest box and entrance hole dimensions for cavity nesting birds vary depending on the size of the bird. If you decide to purchase a manufactured box, remember that commercial boxes are often designed to attract buyers more than birds. Each species has preferred nesting requirements, and the closer you match these preferences, the more likely it is that your nesting structures will attract the tenants you desire. (See chapter five for detailed information on nest boxes.)

LOOSE STONES AND FALLEN LOGS

While many animals are attracted to conspicuous nest boxes, other types of wildlife prefer a more quiet, secretive place to nest, den, or hibernate. Many amphibians, such as frogs and toads, like the cool, moist areas under loose stones and fallen logs. You can provide loose stone simply by leaving such rock features as stepping stones, garden borders, and rock walls uncemented. The rocks will also be used by lizards, butterflies, and perhaps even a turtle or two for coveted basking spots. Fallen logs are especially useful to salamanders and frogs. They can be placed attractively in a number of locations in your garden, and look particularly nice with a few native ferns and perhaps even some volunteer bracket fungi growing on the dark bark.

Songbirds, such as this hermit thrush, need a source of fresh, dependable water.

IRREGULAR CORNERS AND SMALL CREVICES

One final way of creating shelter for wildlife is by locating and preserving choice irregular corners and small crevices around the outside of your home. Some good examples include the loose bark on snags and logs, the space between rocks in a rock wall or garden border, and in the leaf litter. All sorts of wildlife are attracted to these areas, including beneficial insects, earthworms (a Texas gardener's delight), butterflies, turtles, frogs, toads, salamanders, lizards, and small mammals including our enormously beneficial insect-eating bats.

Water

The final critical habitat component to include in a Wildscape is a dependable source of clean water. Many urban and suburbanites forget what a limiting factor water can be in an area that is far from lakes and streams. Because all animals need a source of water, providing a water source in your yard will attract wildlife of all varieties, not just those species that come to feed at your feeders or nest in your nest boxes. Nothing attracts wildlife more effectively on a hot summer day than a supply of cool, fresh water. Vireos, warblers, mockingbirds, cardinals, hummingbirds, bluebirds, orioles, grosbeaks, sparrows, doves, bobwhite, and buntings will flock to your yard. You may also see many varieties of turtles, tadpoles, dragonflies, squirrels, and beetles

using your oasis. If you go a step further and add the sound of moving water by installing a mister, dripper, artificial stream or waterfall, you can almost guarantee that you will attract all sorts of wildlife. The sound of trickling or moving water is an irresistible lure to them. Any extra water feature you add to your basic bird bath or pond will attract a bounty of wildlife.

DESIGNING A BACKYARD POND

A backyard pond does not need to be an elaborate construction. It can be as small as a 1' x 2' depression or as large as an Olympic-sized swimming pool. Before you begin building the pond, though, consider the pond's placement, depth, and the surrounding habitat.

Placement: Locate your pond in an area that receives a good amount of sunlight and is not under a tree or bird feeder. The leaves and seed hulls from trees and feeders will fall into the water and decay, and the decaying material will use up much of the oxygen that is dissolved in the water. When a pond is depleted of oxygen, it becomes stagnant and supports very little aquatic life. Also, make sure the pond is not located in a very low part of the yard where pesticides, fertilizers, and other pollutants will drain into it and collect.

Depth: The depth of the pond is critical. If you want birds to be able to use your pond, leave a sloping area into the pond that has rough or rocky sides

Building a rubber-lined pond involves installing a coping shelf and padding the bottom with sand and other materials.

and bottom and is no more that 2" to 3" deep. This will allow the birds to enter the water, without slipping, to bathe and drink. This is also helpful to small mammals such as squirrels and chipmunks. Provide a nice slope along an edge of the pond for turtles to enter the water and rest on the bank and for the tadpoles and polliwogs to exit their watery habitat. If you wish to include aquatic vegetation (good for a hiding place as well as for frog and toad eggs), be sure to include an area that is 15" to 24" deep.

Surrounding habitat: Plants, particularly flowering ones, in and around your pond will attract more wildlife than a pond with bare edges. However, predators can also lurk in the vegetation surrounding the pond, so include a sunny, grassy bank nearby which small wildlife, such as birds and small mammals, will use. Just outside of pouncing distance but just inside of flitting distance, place a shrub or small tree where birds and other wildlife can hide in case of danger, or simply to dry their feathers or fur. Aesthetically, it is also nice to curve your pond around a corner and camouflage it with native vegetation such as native ornamental grasses or flowering annuals.

BUILDING A BACKYARD POND

Once you have planned the placement, depth, and surrounding habitat of your pond, you are ready to begin building it. Use the following list of steps as guidelines.

one
Use a garden hose or other flexible material to define the outline of your pond, experimenting with a variety of shapes. If you are using a prefabricated liner, use the hose to outline the contours of the liner on the ground.

two
Start digging around the edges of the pond outline. The edge should support a coping shelf, ledge, or lip of the pond. A coping edge made with cement will keep the shelf permanent, and should be dug about 10" or so deep. Later, heavy rocks can be added on top of the shelf to provide a natural look and help keep the shelf from falling or sagging.

three
Once the depth and width of the coping shelf is completed, place 1" x 4" stakes around the perimeter and

FIGURE 3A

FIGURE 3B

Clemente Guzman III

attach "bender board," masonite, or other flexible material to create a wall (figure 3a). This will remind you of a sidewalk being installed.

four
Dig several holes 4" deep around the perimeter of the shelf, close to the center of the distance between the board wall and the earth wall. These can be dug with a post hole digger or a spade shovel.

five
Sink rebar vertically into the holes. Place more sections of rebar around the shelf, tying each horizontal piece to the vertical rebar posts. Horizontal rebar should be a few inches from the ground.

When providing a water element, be sure to create shallow areas for smaller wildlife, such as butterflies, turtles, and songbirds.

FIGURE 3C

six
Add a bit of sand to the bottom before pouring the cement. Sand helps to absorb moisture in the cement and assists with uniform drying of the cement.

seven
Pour the cement into the ditch to form the coping shelf. Level the top of the cement with a flat shovel or straight two-by-four.

eight
Let the cement dry for a day, then remove the board wall and stakes and dig out the center of the pond.

nine
Contour the bottom of the pond to produce specific topographic features (figure 3b). Create a variety of depths for use by different plant and animal life. By sloping the bottom up, you allow gasses that build up under the pond to release without floating (and adding stress to) your liner.

ten
Add a layer of sand to the bottom of the dug-out pond (figure 3c). This helps cushion the bottom of the pond and prevents sharp objects from penetrating the liner. If you have soil that does not drain, or doesn't drain well, you may consider an earth-bottomed pond.

eleven

Prepare your liner. You will want a very thick plastic, such as 45 mil EPDM rubber, which is available at many home repair, garden, and pond specialty shops. Stretch the liner out and repeatedly rinse the side that will face the water. Allow it to dry in the sun for a few hours. Be aware that grass will readily bake under the hot rubber, so if you have any unwanted grass or weeds, this is a good way to get rid of them.

twelve

To figure out how much liner you will need, measure the widest and longest part of the pond. Use the following equations:

Once your pond is finished, add rocks, sand, and flowering plants to complete the scene.

(pond depth x 2)
+ (widest part of the pond)
+ (24 inches "fudge factor")
= *Width*

(pond depth x 2)
+ (longest part of pond)
+ (24 inches "fudge factor")
= *Length*

FIGURE 3D

FIGURE 3E

Clemente Guzman III

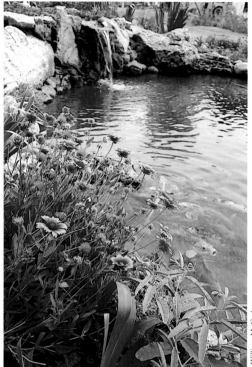

thirteen

Depending on how large your pond is, there are different ways to place your liner into the pond. If you are creating a large pond, simply roll the liner up, carry it to the pond, and unroll it in the pond. Try to conform to the corners and bends of the pond. Use heavy rocks to keep the liner in place as you work. If you have a smaller pond, simply stretch the liner over the top of the pond and hold it in place, suspended over the pond, with rocks. Slowly add water into the center of the liner, which will be pulled down into the pond with the weight of the water. By putting in the liner this way, the liner will automatically curve and pleat to fit the contours of the pond.

fourteen

Fill the pond to the top with water and let it sit for twenty-four hours. This will help you determine if there are any leaks in the liner.

fifteen

Now place the coping material into position. The most often used and most natural-looking coping material is native stone, but be sure that the stone is hard and will not break down in a few years. Place one layer of rocks down first, and puzzle-piece them together. Strive for a good, firm fit so that sun will not break down the liner material. Stack more rocks on top to create the look or height you desire (figure 3d). The rocks should be firmly in place so that the children, who are certain to make a playground out of your Wildscape, will not fall off of an unstable rock.

sixteen

If you would like to add a waterfall or some other moving water element, place a water hose at various sites on the rocks to see where a waterfall would create the most appealing sound to invite wildlife to your newly created pond.

seventeen

Add selected habitat elements to your pond, such as surrounding vegetation (see chapter eleven for suggestions for water plants), water lilies, bog plants, and native aquatic plants (figure 3e). Add Gambusia or goldfish to help with mosquito control; however, fish will eat frog and toad eggs as

FIGURE 3F

well so if you are trying to create a frog pond, wait to add fish until the frog population is firmly established.

eighteen
Trim the liner around the edge of the pond back, or leave it as it is and place small pebbles, rocks, or sand on it to create a little beach (figure 3f). The beach will be used by many animals as a basking area. Birds may even use it as a dust-bathing area. If you slope the beach down into the water, birds will use it for bathing, butterflies will use the margin for "puddling," and turtles will be able to enter and exit the pond with ease.

INSTALLING A PREFORMED POND

When installing a preformed pond, follow the basic plan already outlined, but leave a ledge of about 1" depth to accommodate the lip of the pond form. After digging the pond, place a layer of sand on the bottom of the hole. Use this layer to help level the lowered pond form. Fill the spaces between the pond form and the sides of the soil with earth and/or sand. Let the pond settle for one week before adding other elements such as vegetation or animal life.

© Chuck Kowaleski

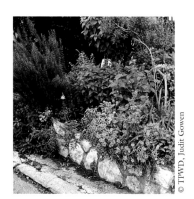

© TPWD, Judit Gowen

Successful Wildscaping involves more than just throwing out a bunch of native plants in your garden. You will need to plan ahead, not only considering the needs of the wildlife you wish to attract, but also the needs of your family. Think of your Wildscape project as a journey. You wouldn't start on a long car trip before checking a map and familiarizing yourself with your route, so take the time to plan for your Wildscape journey as well. It isn't a difficult trip, but it will require a little forethought.

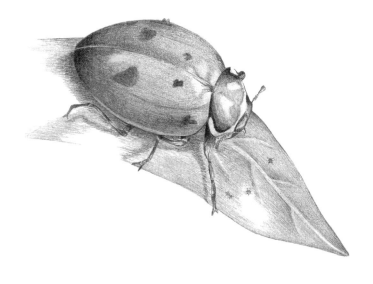

A plan will help you assess your needs and desires and prevent costly mistakes such as installing a pond where you someday want to build a deck. The plan will also help you design a functional habitat to meet the needs of the wildlife you want to attract. Finally, a well-designed plan creates a harmonious, unified garden rather than a piece-meal project. By planning ahead, you can establish your priorities and consider physical and financial limitations.

Design and plan your Wildscape now, and then you can complete the project in stages over several months or years. If your preferences change over time, you can always update and alter your plan to meet your changing needs.

Taking Inventory

To begin your Wildscape plan, take inventory of your yard to determine existing structures, plantings, and environmental conditions. Use the following steps to gather information about your existing yard and sketch the information you gather to form a scaled map (see figures 4a– 4f at the end of this chapter).

one
Determine property dimensions and decide on a scale for your map. Example: $\frac{1}{2}$ in. = 1 ft. Include an arrow pointing north on your map.

two
Show the location of physical features of your property, including the house, garage, storage

A "before" photograph of an un-Wildscaped yard. There's no habitat for colorful songbirds here!

shed, other buildings, driveway, sidewalks, and other hard surfaces on the map to scale. Note locations of doors and windows (figure 4a).

three
Determine possible hazards to gardening, such as utility lines, and mark locations on the map (figure 4b).

four
Add existing vegetation, flower beds, and lawn areas to your landscape plan. Measure trees and large shrubs from the middle of the trunk out to the tip of a branch to estimate tree spread and mark these on your map. Note any plants that affect energy conservation and comfort in your home such as shade trees and windbreaks.

five
Mark down environmental conditions. Show soil conditions and areas that are sunny, shady, wet, dry, windy, or sloped.

six
Identify special wildlife features such as feeding areas, tree cavities, thick cover, or water sources.

seven
Show neighboring property features that have an effect on your yard, such as roads, fences, noisy pets, or overhanging trees.

eight
Make several copies of your scaled inventory map to use throughout the planning stages.

Evaluating Current Use

Once you have completed your property inventory, you can evaluate what you have to work with and how these features are currently being used. You need to consider current usage by both your family and wildlife in the area. Using one copy of your inventory map, sketch in circular areas to represent family, service, and wildlife use to construct a "current use" map.

Many birds, such as this Eastern Screech Owl, require a cavity in which to nest.

FAMILY NEEDS

Consider how you and your family currently use your yard to determine your family needs. What activities do you and your family enjoy that involve your yard? Do you entertain friends on the patio? Do your children like to play in the yard?

SERVICE AREAS

Service areas include the storage shed, garbage can storage, firewood stack, air conditioning units, garden shed, and vegetable garden. Do these areas need to be shaded, open, accessible? Would you prefer that they be hidden? How close do they need to be to the primary residence?

WILDLIFE CONSIDERATIONS

Since the primary object of Wildscapes is to attract native wildlife to your yard, think about the wildlife already utilizing your property. How does wildlife use your yard now? Where does wildlife congregate in your yard? What types of wildlife visit? View your yard from an animal's perspective. What does your yard provide now in terms of food, water, cover, and travel corridors?

Evaluating Future Needs

After finishing the property inventory and current use assessment, you can begin to decide future uses for your property. This is an opportunity to create the yard you have always wanted—on paper at least. Using another copy of your inventory map and referring to your current use map, plan your "future use" map by sketching in tentative ideas and notes (figure 4c). Include locations of your water sources, brush or rock piles, bird feeders, or other wildlife features you plan to add (figure 4d). While you brainstorm, consider the following future use of public, private, service areas.

PUBLIC AREAS

Public areas are visible to the public and may be accessed by people other than your family. What are your future plans for public areas around your yard? Does your front yard need a more manicured look to conform to neighborhood standards? Can it have islands of color for hummingbirds and butterflies? Do you need additional trees or shrubs?

PRIVATE AREAS

Private areas are designated spaces for family use, such as the patio, deck, or backyard. Where do you need privacy screens? What are the desirable views from your windows? Do you need more shade over the back patio? Would you like to reduce yard maintenance and mowing by decreasing the amount of lawn? Do you need designated children's play areas?

SERVICE AREAS

Will your service areas alter with changes in the yard? Do you need more room or can you scale down the space designated to these areas? Plan adequate access to these areas and consider ways to screen them from direct view.

Designing for Function

Before selecting plants for your Wildscape, think of the "big picture." Plants are more than pretty, they are also functional, providing shelter, nesting areas, and source of food (nectar, fruit, nuts, and berries). Consider your future plants' functions and how and where they can best be utilized in your yard.

one
Starting at one corner of your "future use" map, sketch in beds and rough shapes to represent general types of plants you want (to scale) considering how they will function to attract wildlife (figure 4e).

two
As you work, refer to your "current use" map. Think about your needs such as privacy hedging, shade, flowing trees, or understory shrubs and include them on the map.

three
Sketch in locations of your water sources, brush or rock piles, bird feeders, or other wildlife features you plan to add.

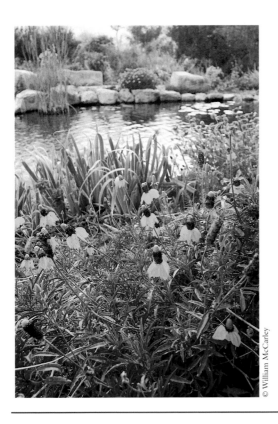

© TPWD, Chuck Kowaleski

DESIGN TIPS

one
Curves replicate nature better than straight lines. Curved lines fool your eyes to make spaces seem larger or more distant.

two
Disguise boundaries. A small space looks more confined when its edges are obvious. Use vines or shrubs to soften the straight lines of a fence, or use open fencing materials, such as chain link, split rail, or lattice.

three
Colors affect your perception of space. Cool colors (blue, green, violet) retreat visually to give the impression of greater space. Warm colors (yellow, red, orange) seem to surge forward, making the space look small. If you plant warm and cool colors together, use four times more cool color to balance the warm.

four
Growers define "full sun" as six hours or more of direct sunlight daily, including four hours of hot afternoon sun. "Full shade" is defined as four hours or less of direct sunlight per day. "Partial sun" and "partial shade" fall somewhere in between. (For information on predominately shady yards, see chapter eleven.)

five
Remember to design your yard vertically with layers of vegetation, including trees, shrubs, and groundcovers. Place shorter plants in the foreground with taller plants in the background.

© William McCarley

six

If you are looking for shade in some areas, consider planting a few fast growing, short-lived trees mixed together with slow growing, longer-lived trees.

SELECTING PLANTS

Choosing plants for your Wildscape is not as difficult as it may seem, but does take some thought. Having already chosen the general types of plants for your plan, you are ready to select specific plants to accomplish your objectives.

one

Concentrate on plants native to Texas that provide food and shelter for wildlife. Remember that not every plant native to Texas is adapted to your area. Refer to the range map (figure 2a, page 11) and chapter two to determine the ecological region in which you are located and the plants and growing conditions that are typical for your area.

two

Study your Wildscape plan to establish your planting needs. Begin thinking about specific plants that serve each function. See the native plants table in the appendix for suggested plants suitable for your region.

three

Refer to your inventory map to check existing light, water, and soil conditions. Make sure to choose plants that are appropriate for those areas.

four

Consider each plant's mature height and width, hardiness, color, and blooming and fruiting period during plant selection. Remember to create layers of vegetation.

five

Note interesting features about each plant. Be aware of potential problems associated with each plant, such as sap or pollen that might cause allergies, leaves or berries that might be poisonous to children or pets, maintenance problems such as messy fruit or invasive roots, or aggressive plants that may grow out of control.

Planning and planting a Wildscape is a wonderful activity in which to include children.

six

Once you have identified specific plant species for each area, use another copy of your base map to write in the actual plants that will accomplish the functions you determined (figure 4f).

Design Checklist

Before beginning actual work on your Wildscape make sure your design plan includes:

- ✔ Native plants
- ✔ Water source (shallow areas, reliable)
- ✔ Plant diversity
- ✔ Winter shelter
- ✔ Layers of vegetation
- ✔ Snags or nest boxes
- ✔ Year-round food sources
- ✔ Optimal viewing spots for your family

The Importance of Soil

Soils are the foundation of life. They serve as an anchor for plant roots and are the storehouse for the nutrients, organic matter, air, and water needed for plant growth. Good soils will grow healthy and vigorous plants, which will, in turn, produce an abundance of food and cover for a wide array of wildlife. Knowing what type of soil you have and how to condition it can help you plan and plant a successful Wildscape.

Texas is blessed with a wonderful variety of soils. They are different in mineral composition, particle size, organic matter, pH, and even color. But all good, healthy soils are a dynamic mixture and balance of air, water, minerals, organic matter, and living organisms. The destruction of this balance through the relatively recent agricultural practices of applying harsh synthetic fertilizers and chemicals and removal of dead organic matter has reduced our living soils to dry, sterile dirt.

Before you prepare your soil for your Wildscape plants, you may wish to determine its chemical characteristics by having it tested. The tester should be a company which will give you detailed information about your soil's chemical composition as well as organic fertilizer recommendations. Local nurseries or Texas AgriLife Extension offices may be able to furnish this service.

PREPARING YOUR SOIL

To begin replenishing the health and vigor of your soils, concentrate on two main components of the soil: air and humus. Air is extremely important for soil health, for without it, humus formation cannot occur. To increase the air in your soil, turn the soil mechanically with a hand cultivator for ornamental beds, use a mechanical aerator for lawns, or rip or

By installing a Wildscape, you automatically reduce the amount of time, money, and chemicals necessary to maintain the health and beauty of your garden.

chisel plow larger acreage. Encourage or introduce earthworms to your gardens, as they will provide both the necessary components of air and humus. Humus is the dead, decaying organic matter in the soil which acts as a water reservoir and a slow-release plant food. The best source of humus for lawn and garden is compost. Apply four to six inches of compost over new gardens and watch your soil and plants come alive. By correcting your soil's aeration and humus content, the other elements of healthy soil (microorganisms and chemical nutrients) will naturally be improved.

DETERMINING YOUR SOIL TYPE

The soils of Texas are often described in a variety of terms, which can sometimes be confusing. The most common soil types of Texas include:

Sand: Sandy soil is soil that readily accepts water and that readily releases water. Plant roots grow easily through sandy soil, and can find oxygen pockets even when the soil is wet. The pH of most sandy soil is neutral or acidic, and therefore acid-loving plants such as flowering dogwood and pine will thrive in it. In areas of low rainfall such as South and West Texas, though, sandy soil will be slightly alkaline.

Loam: Loam is a mixture of sand and clay soils, which also contains a hefty amount of organic matter. This combination is the ideal soil which will grow just about anything. Loam is generally neutral or slightly acidic.

Clay: Clay soils are dense, heavy soils. You may also have heard this soil referred to as "gumbo," especially in the Houston area. This is the thick, gummy stuff that will suck your boots off when its wet and be rock hard when it is dry. Most prairie plants do very well in clay soil. Do not try to keep your clay soil consistently wet, as it will literally suffocate sand and loam loving plants. Wet areas that receive more than forty-five inches of rainfall annually will have slightly acid clay soils. With less rainfall, the soil will be slightly alkaline.

An excellent source of information and recommendations on organic gardening and soil health is *The Dirt Doctor's Guide to Organic Gardening* by J. Howard Garrett.

Maintaining a Wildscape

Maintenance of your newly planted Wildscape is vital for success. Through regular maintenance, you will become familiar with the vital ecosystem developing in your yard. The good news is that by using native plants you have already reduced the long-term maintenance required, but your new plants will need your assistance most during the first year or two.

WATER
Even drought-resistant plants must have water. Whether from rain or your garden hose, your newly planted Wildscape will need regular watering for the first few years. As plants begin to mature, consider infrequent but deep watering, then water only in periods of extreme stress. Remember to water only in the early morning or later evening to reduce water loss through evaporation. Slow watering below the bottom leaves, perhaps with a soaker hose or drip irrigation system, will discourage molds and some diseases and garden pests.

MULCHING
Mulching conserves water, adds humus and nutrients to the soil, discourages weeds, and gives your beds a nice, finished appearance. Flower beds and trees should have a 3" blanket of roughly-shredded wood or other organic material. Continue to add a layer of aged mulch to your Wildscape beds and around bases of trees each year. Avoid placing freshly shredded material around your plants. This fresh mulch may be too acidic and will be in a "hot stage" of decomposition which can actually burn your plants. Allow the mulch to compost in a pile for a few months before adding it to your Wildscape. A layer of pine needles can be applied around acid-loving plants each fall.

FERTILIZERS
A good application of mulch should take care of the nutrients your plants require and therefore reduce the need for fertilizers. In fact, many native plants dislike chemical fertilizers and grow better without fertilizers of any kind. If you decide your plants need fertilizing, one application of an organic fertilizer to the soil before the growing season begins should be sufficient.

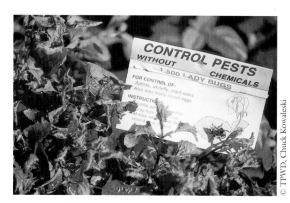

Many people buy beneficial insects, such as these ladybugs, to help control pests in their garden.

MOWING
Wildflower patches look beautiful while blooming, but may look "weedy" when the flowers have gone to seed. Mow the wildflower patch with the mower blade four to six inches above the ground after the spring bloomers have dropped their seeds. This allows the summer and fall bloomers to continue growing while trimming the spent stalks. In some areas, you may want to allow the spent flower heads to remain since birds enjoy the seeds over the winter.

PRUNING
Native plants may need occasional trimming to remove damaged branches or maintain proper shape. Prune only those branches which are rubbing other branches and causing injury, broken and damaged limbs, diseased limbs, limbs with mistletoe, dangerous limbs, and suckers. Avoid pruning trees during the first year in order to allow them time to become established. In February, trim off the stalks of perennials which die down to the ground each winter and wait for the plant to resprout from the roots in the spring. Or, by leaving the stalk in place over the winter, you allow the seeds to scatter and supply birds with a winter food source. Other perennials die back to the ground and overwinter (survive the winter) as a small rosette of green leaves. Try not to disturb these green clumps through the winter. You will be rewarded with colorful blooms in the spring.

PEST MANAGEMENT
Controlling pests in your Wildscape involves different strategies to maintain the health of your backyard ecosystem. Integrated pest management combines

A Wildscape is a beautiful and beneficial addition to any area, no matter how large or small.

the use of natural predators, proper plant selection, and other biological and chemical methods to discourage pests. Wildscaping encourages respect for all aspects of nature. The presence of insects in your Wildscape shows that you have been successful in attracting a key component of the food web. Birds, such as the mockingbird, purple martin, and woodpecker, feed on these insects. Other creatures, including ladybugs, frogs, lizards, spiders, and bats also eat insects. By leaving the insects in your Wildscape, you are maintaining a reliable food source for those insectivorous wildlife species.

The most important step in pest management is to maintain healthy soil. Good, healthy soil produces healthy plants which are better able to withstand plant diseases and insect damage. The second step is plant selection, with emphasis on hardy plants. Native plant species are generally less susceptible to native insect damage and disease. The third step is diligence and active warfare. By frequently observing your plants, you can conquer insect problems in the early states. Nontoxic methods of insect control include manually removing the pests, spraying them with strong jets of water, and maintaining or releasing native beneficial predatory insect populations. Use soapy water, insecticide soap, diatomaceous earth, pyrethrum, and BT bacteria as alternatives to more conventional insecticides, but do so judiciously. By avoiding the use of insecticides, you are also protecting the butterflies and caterpillars residing in your Wildscape. Learn to recognize the caterpillars, ladybugs, and other desirable invertebrates visiting your Wildscape.

COMPOSTING

Compost is an integral part of your Wildscape. Compost improves soil structure, texture, and aeration and increases the soil's water holding capacity. Compost loosens clay soils and helps sandy soils retain water. Adding compost promotes soil fertility and stimulates healthy root development in plants.

To create compost, you will need equal amounts of "browns" and "greens." Browns are dry materials, such as dried leaves, wood chips, and small twigs. Greens are fresh, moist materials, such as grass clippings, weeds, and food scraps. Avoid using woody stalks, large branches, pet excrement, fats, and meats. These items will take much longer to decompose and may attract nuisance animals. Make sure to keep your compost moist. A good rule of thumb is to keep the material as moist as a wrung out sponge. Composting may take a month to a year, depending on the amount of aeration, moisture, and composting materials you use. Turning compost is necessary to ensure proper aeration, which promotes aerobic decomposition. Turn the compost once a week or whenever you add new material. To contain the compost material, construct your own container by surrounding it with chicken wire or other open mesh fencing, enclosing three sides with hay bales or wooden pallets, or simply heaping the material in a pile. You can also purchase one of several styles of composting bins on the market. For additional composting information, contact the Texas Commission on Environmental Quality, the Texas AgriLife Extension Service in your county, Native Plant Society, Texas Master Gardeners, or any of the proactive municipal composting programs found throughout Texas. Your city or town may also have composting programs which will provide you with information.

street

16 feet   22 feet   42 feet

driveway

sidewalk

house

130 feet   130 feet

garage   patio

busy street

100 feet

ditch

1 small square = 2 feet

FIGURE 4A

Base map of your property, showing dimensions and buildings to scale.

Source: Designing a Wildscape, *Diana Foss, Texas Parks and Wildlife, 1997.*

street

N

overhead lines

phone

full sun

underground plumbing

live oak
shady

azaleas   azaleas

house

chain link fence

neighbor's yard
noisy, dogs

best
views

nc

garage   patio

firewood   lilies

ligustrum
lilies

lilies

live oak
shady

wooden fence

busy street

lawn

full sun

low area
poor drainage
clay soil

X bird feeder

slopes

slopes

O snag

sandy soil

chain link fence

ditch

1 small square = 2 feet

FIGURE 4B

*Inventory map of your property, including existing vegetation,
environmental conditions, potential gardening hazards, and
other special features.*

Source: Designing a Wildscape, *Diana Foss, Texas Parks and
Wildlife, 1997.*

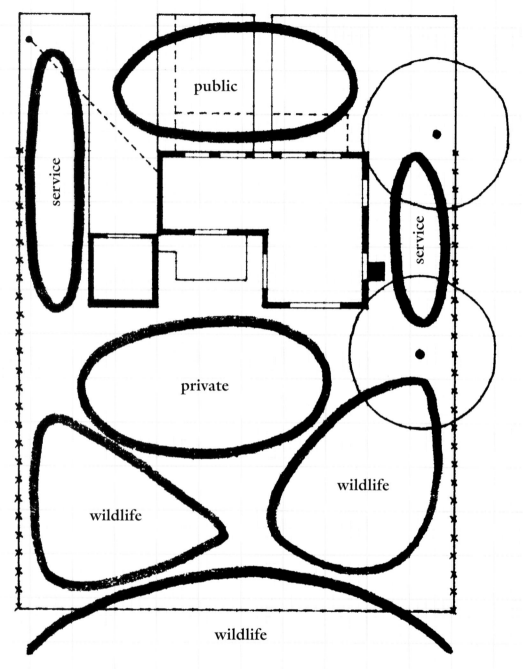

N

public

service

service

private

wildlife

wildlife

wildlife

1 small square = 2 feet

FIGURE 4C

Future uses sketched on a copy of the base map. Try various layouts on paper (see figure 4d).

Source: Designing a Wildscape, *Diana Foss, Texas Parks and Wildlife, 1997.*

1 small square = 2 feet

FIGURE 4D

Future uses sketched on a copy of the base map. Try various layouts on paper (see figure 4c).

Source: Designing a Wildscape, *Diana Foss, Texas Parks and Wildlife, 1997.*

FUTURE GOALS:

1. Add trees to front yard.
2. Reduce yard in back and add wildlife area.
3. Shade the play area.
4. Add vegetable garden and screen from view.
5. Screen fences with vines and shrubs.
6. Leave dying tree as snag.
7. Add other wildlife features, such as brush pile, purple martin house, and rock wall.
8. Add pond near seating area.
9. Replace lilies and ligustrum with colorful nectar plants.

1 small square = 2 feet

FIGURE 4E

Wildscape plan focusing on the function of each plant, rather than individual species.

Source: Designing a Wildscape, *Diana Foss, Texas Parks and Wildlife, 1997.*

Figure 4f Legend

NECTAR SOURCES

N	Black-eyed Susan	MBS	Mealy Blue Sage
C	Clematis Vine	N	Mexican Hat
CR	Cross-vine	N	Mexican Milkweed
N	Indian Blanket	N	Mistflower
N	Katie's Ruellia	N	Scarlet Sage
	Lantana, New Gold	T	Turk's Cap
	Lantana, Texas	N	Verbena

WILDLIFE AREA

groundcovers		trees	
Partridgeberry		CL	Cherry Laurel
Wood Violets		FT	Fringe Tree
		MP	Mexican Plum
shrubs		PH	Parsley Hawthorn
BB	American Beautyberry	PS	Persimmon
	Coralberry	P	Possumhaw
DC	Dwarf Cherry Laurel	MB	Red Mulberry
V	Rusty Blackhaw	RDW	Rough-leaf Dogwood
	Viburnum	SCO	Swamp Chestnut Oak
		SB	Sweet Bay Magnolia

SCREENING

CH	Coral Honeysuckle	PV	Passionflower Vine
DWM	Dwarf Wax Myrtle		Southern Wax Myrtle

POND AREA

Buttonbush	Lizard's-tail
Cardinal Flower	Louisiana Iris
False Indigo	Obedient Plant
Gulf Coast Penstemon	Swamp Lily
Halberd-leaf Hibiscus	Swamp Sunflower
Horsetail	Water-lily

MISCELLANEOUS

AZ	Existing Azalea Bushes	FW	Firewood
▲	Bat House	■	Purple Martin House
	Bench		Vine Trellis
X	Bird Feeder	○	Snag
✱	Brush Pile		

1 small square = 2 feet

FIGURE 4F

Wildscape plan for a Houston home, featuring specific plants that perform the functions specified in figure 4e. See legend at right.

Source: Designing a Wildscape, *Diana Foss, Texas Parks and Wild-life, 1997.*

Part 2
GARDENING TIPS FOR TEXAS CRITTERS

© TPWD

© Teaming With Wildlife

Since the dawn of human existence, birds have evoked wonder and a sense of mystery. Perhaps with no other creature has our relationship been so constant, so varied, and so enriched by art, symbol, and myth as has our relationship with birds. They dazzle us with their beauty, fascinate us with their antics, and charm us with their varied and melodious songs. Their command on our imagination is not really so surprising. Because they have the ability to fly away from predators, many birds allow humans to observe them at relatively close range and for long periods of time. Happily, it is easy to attract these beauties to a backyard garden. Curious to the extreme, birds are ever on the lookout for dependable feeding opportunities, a place to quench their thirst or bathe, a quick rest stop on a longer journey, and, for some, a safe place to build a nest and raise their young.

Providing for the birds is easy, and you can make your garden more attractive to them in a variety of ways. The key to success is to offer the proper combination of the avian amenities of food, water, and shelter. With planning, it may require only a few additions or changes to transform your yard into an oasis for the birds.

Creating a "Bird-friendly" Yard

one
Make a literal "bird's-eye view" inventory of your yard; you may already have a number of native trees, shrubs, and flowers attractive to various species of birds. Oaks, cedars, sycamores, elms, and hackberries provide the architecture of a fine habitat. They also furnish food, cover, and nesting sites.

two
Supplement with a wide selection of native fruiting trees, shrubs, and vines. Plants that bear fruit and berries are particularly alluring to bluebirds, cardinals, and mockingbirds in the summer, not to mention cedar waxwings and robins in the winter. Favorites include Ashe juniper, yaupon, deciduous holly, viburnum, elderberry, lance-leaf and evergreen sumacs, Mexican plum, Virginia creeper, rough-leaf dogwood, and red mulberry.

three
Create a layered and multi-tiered effect, increase edge, and provide a rich understory. This will

A thick, lush understory has attracted this American robin.

increase bird species diversity. Ground-nesters and birds that nest in low, thick shrubs may consider your garden as a potential site to raise their young.

four
Make sure to provide ample clean water. A formal bird bath or even an overturned garbage can top will do. A dripping system that makes a gurgling sound is highly attractive to passing birds. We all know that water is essential for life, but it also provides an area for bathing, which is important to feather maintenance. Elevating the bird bath helps protect birds from cats and other predators. Provide cover and perch sites nearby for quick getaways and places to hide from predators, such as cats and hawks.

five
Reduce the area occupied by the lawn. Wide expanses of turf grass are sterile habitats attracting less desirable "generalist" species, such as feral pigeons, starlings, cowbirds, and grackles.

Creating proper habitat for birds will encourage them to stay for more than just dinner!

Berries like these from a deciduous yaupon (Ilex decidua) will feed birds during the lean winter times.

six

Provide splashes of color in different areas of the garden. Birds, like butterflies, are highly visual creatures and are attracted by brightly colored wildflowers and fruit. Those glitzy hummingbirds are especially fond of red and orange tubular flowers. Red salvias, penstemons, standing cypress, trumpet creeper, and flame acanthus will draw a bevy of birds, especially during migration.

seven

Use native grasses as accent plants and in wildlife meadow patches. House finches, painted buntings, goldfinches, native sparrows, and doves readily eat seeds of native grasses and composites, such as sunflowers. Also, consider letting your garden flowers go to seed. Doing so provides a wealth of nutritious food for many species of seed-eating birds.

eight

Reduce or avoid the use of pesticides in your yard. Many insecticides remove all insects, including beneficial insects as well as pests, that serve as the prey base for insectivorous birds. Using plants native to your region reduces the need for pesticide use since the native plants are resistant to local pests and diseases. Besides, let your birds do the pest control. Mockingbirds, warblers, vireos, and wrens relish insect pests and gobble them up with fervor.

nine

Supplement with feeders. There are several styles of feeders on the market that cater to the tastes of different species of birds: nectar feeders for hummingbirds, tubular feeders for chickadees and titmice, platforms feeders for cardinals, house finches, and white-crowned sparrows, suet feeders for woodpeckers and other winter insectivores, and impaled oranges and other fruit for orioles, mockingbirds, and other fruit mongers. Keep your feeders clean and dry. Seed feeders that get wet often harbor mold and bacteria which can be harmful or fatal to birds, and feeders that are not cleaned regularly will spread avian diseases.

ten

Protect your birds from feral and domestic cats. Your beloved cat, no matter how well fed, plays havoc with newly-fledged birds—and their parents, too. It is unfair to attract birds to your yard if you have cats on the prowl.

eleven

Resist removing large old trees with cavities. These standing dead trees, or snags, are used by woodpeckers who make their nests in the soft wood. Many other species of birds, including chickadees, titmice, some flycatchers, and bluebirds, depend on deserted woodpecker holes to raise their young. If there are very few snags in your area, consider putting up a few nest boxes.

© TPWD, John Herron

Birds are attuned to the sound of water. By providing fresh, clean, and dependable water, you can attract a variety of bird life.

one

Build the house for a specific species (figure 5a) with the proper entrance size, cavity depth, and height (see table 5.1 at the end of this chapter).

two

Use ¾" durable woods like cypress, cedar, redwood or exterior-grade plywood as building materials. Avoid pressure-treated lumber or wood with green or yellow-tinted preservatives, since these preservatives may release toxins.

three

Avoid using plastic or metal boxes, which become lethally hot in Texas summers.

four

When building nest boxes, attach the boards using wood screws, or concrete-coated or ring-shank nails. Galvanized nails tend to loosen as wood expands and contracts.

five

Build a wooden roof extending over all sections of the house for maximum protection.

six

To help birds climb out of the box, provide cleats or roughen the surface beneath the entrance hole with a wood chisel.

© TPWD, Judit Gowen

A proper backyard bird habitat will have a dependable source of water, multi-layered vegetation, and a variety of food sources including flowering and fruiting trees, shrubs, and forbs, and even supplemental feeders.

seven

To provide ventilation, leave gaps between the roof and sides of the box, or drill a few $\frac{1}{4}$" holes in the sides just below the roof. To ensure proper drainage, cut the corners off the floor or drill $\frac{1}{4}$" holes in the box floor.

eight

Provide an easy way to clean out the box.

© TPWD, John Herron

A variety of birds can be attracted to seed feeders. This American goldfinch is enjoying black oil sunflower seed from a hanging feeder. They also love thistle seeds.

FIGURE 5A

Clemente Guzman III

Eastern bluebird returning to the nestbox to feed hungry nestlings. Nestboxes can be a valuable commodity to cavity nesting species.

nine

Except for purple martin houses, most nest boxes do not need to be painted. Paint purple martin houses white (on the outside only) to increase chances of house occupation. If you do paint other boxes, choose muted colors that blend in with the natural environment, and don't stain houses with materials like creosote or lead-based paint. If you need to apply a waterproofing agent, apply only on the outside.

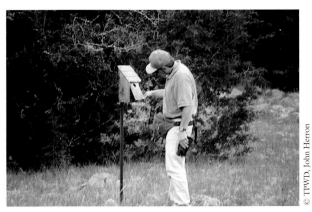

It is essential to provide an easy method to clean out and monitor nestboxes. You will need to clean out nest parasites, old nesting material, and invasive exotic species such as house sparrows or European starlings.

ten

Don't provide perches, since starlings and house sparrows often take over houses with this accessory. (For more methods of deterring pests and predators, see chapter ten.)

eleven

Monitor nest boxes for signs of house sparrow or European starling occupation, and promptly evict these invasive, exotic species. To deter wasps from building in the box, coat the ceiling of the box with bar soap. If you notice blowfly larvae infesting the nest, gently lift up the nest and tap out the insects, brushing the pests out of the box before lowering the nest. To deter ants, coat a section of the post or pole with axle grease, petroleum jelly, or Tanglefoot™. Be sure to wrap the section of post with tape before applying grease.

twelve

Houses mounted on metal poles are less vulnerable to predators than houses nailed to wood posts or trees. Clear tall vegetation from the base, and wrap sheet metal around wooden poles to deter predators from climbing into boxes.

thirteen

Use no more than four small nest boxes for any one species or one large box per acre. Separate bluebird houses by 100 yards, and do not put any houses near bird feeders. In areas with hot summers, face the entrance holes of your boxes north or east to avoid overheating the box.

Table 5.1
NEST BOX REQUIREMENTS
(MEASUREMENTS IN INCHES EXCEPT WHERE INDICATED)

Species	Floor	Depth	Entrance height above floor	Entrance diameter	Height above ground (feet)	Habitat
Eastern Bluebird	5x5	8	6	$1\frac{1}{2}$	5	Short grassy areas, with scattered trees for perches.
Carolina Chickadee	4x4	8–10	6–8	$1\frac{1}{8}$	4–15	Yards, etc., with mature hardwood trees, 40%–60% sunlight.
Carolina Wren	4x4	6–8	1–6	$1\frac{1}{2}$	6–10	Open deciduous woodland, especially with good cover, farmland, and suburbs.
House Wren	4x4	8–10	1–6	$1\frac{1}{4}$	6–10	Wooded, shrubby habitats. Place box under eaves or in a tree.
Bewick's Wren	4x4	8–10	6–8	$1 – 1\frac{1}{4}$	6–15	Open woodland, shrubland, farmland, and suburbs.
Tufted Titmouse	4x4	8–10	6–8	$1\frac{1}{4}$	6–15	Woodlands and forests including parks.
Red-headed Woodpecker	6x6	12	10	2	10–20	Open woods, farmlands, bottomlands, parks, and backyards. Place wood chips in box.
Golden-fronted Woodpecker	6x6	12–15	9–12	2	12–20	Dry woodlands, pecan groves, mesquite brushlands, towns, and parks.
Ladder-backed Woodpecker	6x6	12–15	9–12	$1\frac{1}{2}$	12–20	Dry country including brushlands, mesquite, and cactus, often associated with towns and rural areas. Place wood chips in box.
Downy Woodpecker	4x4	9–12	6–8	$1\frac{1}{4}$	6–20	Will nest in deciduous and mixed conifer woodlands, riparian woodlands, orchards, and parks. Place wood chips in box.
Northern Flicker	7x7	16–18	14–16	$1\frac{1}{2}$	6–20	Open woodlands and suburban areas.
Barn Owl	10x18	15–18	4	6	12–18	Mixed agricultural land: meadows, haylands, and pastures

Species	Floor	Depth	Entrance height above floor	Entrance diameter	Height above ground (feet)	Habitat
Eastern Screech Owl	8x8	12–15	9–12	3	10–30	Variety: woodlots, forests, swamps, orchards, parks, suburban gardens, especially edges. Use 2–3" wood chips in box.
Wood Duck	10x18	10–24	12–16	4(w)x3(h)	10–20	Bottomland woodlands and wetlands. Place 4" cedar shavings in box.
Black-bellied Whistling Duck	10x18	10–24	12–16	4	10–20	Trees near woodland streams, ponds, and marshes of South Texas.
American Robin	6x8	8	nesting shelf	nesting shelf	6–15	Nests under eaves or soffits of buildings, or on top of light fixtures. Also in trees and shrubs.
Barn Swallow	6x6	6	nesting shelf	nesting shelf	8–12	Farmsteads, on rafters, under eaves, or on top of light fixtures
Purple Martin	6x6	6	1	$2\frac{1}{2}$	15–20	Form colonies. Place boxes in open area, at least 30' away from trees, and preferably near open water.
Eastern Phoebe	6x6	6	nesting shelf	nesting shelf	8–12	Build mud-pellet nests in a variety of human-built structures, especially beneath bridges, in culverts, wells, and under eaves and soffets.
Great-crested Flycatcher	6x6	8–10	6–8	$1\frac{9}{16}$	8–20	Hardwood forests, orchards, and parks. Prefer pines, mixed conifers, or hardwood stands. Sometimes uses nest boxes.
Ash-throated Flycatcher	6x6	8–10	6–8	$1\frac{1}{2}$	8–20	Variety: deserts, chaparral, and woodlands.
Prothonotary Warbler	6x6	6	4	$1\frac{1}{2}$	3–5 above surface of water	Bottomland hardwood forests. Nests in flooded backwater habitats, in snags above water, or facing water.

© TPWD, Kelly Bryan

© TPWD

Over 600 species of birds have been recorded in Texas. The diversity of Texas' habitats, as well as its vast size, account for this phenomenon. The following are a few of the more common and best-loved species of the state that may visit your Wildscape.

NORTHERN MOCKINGBIRD
Mimus polyglottos

© TPWD

Texas' state bird, the mocking-bird, is a talented mimic.

A feisty defender of home territory, this vociferous mimic will often nest in shrubs and trees near your home. Sometimes known to sing by the light of the full moon, or even bright streetlights, the Texas state bird is a great lover of fruit and will defend a berry-laden shrub from all who would dare to trespass. The northern mockingbird is perhaps best known for its singing abilities. Not only can it perform thirty-nine species' songs and fifty call notes, but it can also mimic sounds such as a barking dog, squeaky hinges, notes from a piano, and even a cackling hen. The mocking-bird performs so expertly that even an electronic analysis cannot tell the difference between the mockingbird and the original source of the sound. The medium-sized songbird is dull gray above with paler under-parts, and is easily identified by the flash of white produced in flight by its wings and outer tail feathers.

Though territorial all year, mockingbirds are especially aggressive during the nesting season, which falls between March and August. If they feel threatened, they may attack starlings, grackles, and even cats. Nests are a bulky cup constructed of dry leaves, stems, cotton, paper, grass, and other handy materials. Females incubate the three to six blue or green eggs, which are spotted with brown. Incubation lasts from eleven to fourteen days, and the young leave the nest after they are ten to twelve days old.

The northern mockingbird is widely distributed and has extended its range much farther north in recent years. They range throughout North America from southern Canada south to Mexico, and have even been introduced and established in Hawaii. Mockingbirds live in Texas all year round and they frequent lawns and gardens in urban and rural environments, edges of open woods, farm-land, streamside thickets, and brushy deserts.

SCISSOR-TAILED FLYCATCHER
Tyrannus forficatus

© TPWD, Glen Mills

The beautiful and acrobatic scissor-tailed flycatcher is one of Texans' favorite birds.

Despite being the state bird of Oklahoma, the scis-sor-tailed flycatcher probably ranks number one as Texans' favorite bird. Its great beauty and aerial maneuvers make it a marvel to behold. On their summer breeding grounds they are birds of open country, where scattered shrubs and trees serve as convenient lookout perches. Males will valiantly defend their territory from crows, caracaras, ravens, hawks, and other birds much larger than them-selves. Often seen perched on telephone wires, they seem oblivious to passing traffic.

Males and females are generally similar in appearance, females being slightly smaller with shorter tails. Upper parts are pearly gray while underparts are whitish with salmon pink sides. The male performs one of the most spectacu-lar courtship displays imaginable as he wheels and dives in an elaborate sky ballet to attract the female's attention. For all the intensity of the courtship display, these birds make little fuss about their nest.

One of Texas' most popular and beautiful birds, the scissor-tailed flycatcher is the state bird of Oklahoma.

Females lay five creamy eggs in bulky nests which are placed about fifteen feet high in isolated trees. Scissor-tailed flycatchers winter from Mexico south to Panama. During the fall migration, motorists may count hundreds perched on telephone wires.

CHUCK-WILL'S-WIDOW
Caprimulgus carolinensis

The long, mournful song of the Chuck-will's-widow has lulled countless rural Texans to sleep.

Our largest nightjar (a family of long-winged, nocturnal birds), this southern cousin of the whippoor-will used to be fairly common through most of the eastern two-thirds of Texas. Mottled buff-brown overall with a long tail and rounded wings,

its intricate plumage serves as a perfect camouflage. The male differs from the female in having white on the end of the outer tail feathers and a poorly-defined white band across the lower throat. The Chuck-will's-widow is active mainly after dark. Named for its call, this persistent singer seems to clearly pronounce its name: *Chuck, Will's wid-ow.* While hunting, it is also known to utter an eerie growl or croak.

Most feeding is done on the wing, close to the ground, with silent flight. Preferred food consists of beetles and moths that the bird scoops out of the air as it flies the night skies with its mouth wide open. A very effective feeding mechanism, its 2-inch-wide gape is lined with a fringe of stiff bristles that act as a funnel. It will also occasionally take small birds during migration, including hummingbirds, swallows, and warblers. By day, it spends most of its time crouching on or near a fallen log, on a horizontal limb, or on the leaf litter blanketing the forest floor. The female builds no nest but lays two eggs directly on the ground in the leaf litter. She lures predators away from the eggs by feigning injury. If the eggs are disturbed, the female will pick each one up in her mouth and transfer it to a safer location—an unusual behavior in birds. This chunky nightjar winters from Cuba, the Bahamas, and Guatemala south to northern Columbia. Sadly, this nighttime songster, which is heard more often than seen, is being heard less and less. Ground nesting birds are very vulnerable to the increased numbers of predators, especially house cats, found in fragmented woodland habitats. Outright loss of habitat has also taken its toll.

The beauty of the blue jay is often overlooked. Commonly found in eastern Texas gardens, the jay is a noisy and boisterous inhabitant.

BLUE JAY
Cyanocitta cristata

Sometimes a mischievous rascal, this robin-sized blue and white bird with the jaunty crest is a frequent inhabitant of suburban gardens. In wilder places, they still dwell in woodlands along streams and groves of trees on prairies. In Texas, blue jays occur mainly in the eastern half of the state. Exuberant and raucous, the blue jay is mostly a vegetarian, feeding on acorns, nuts, seeds, and fruit. Some of these nuts are not eaten immediately but "cached" in the ground for use later. Blue jays will also glean a variety of insects, some spiders, and other small invertebrates from tree limbs and branches. Not particularly shy, this wily bird will often lord over the other birds at the feeder, supplanting smaller foragers when the opportunity arises. They are also known to periodically help themselves to the contents of any unguarded nests they happen to encounter.

Except during the breeding season, jays tend to troop noisily through parks and woodlands in loose bands. Oddly, you will often see jays "mobbing" large predatory birds such as crows, hawks, and owls. A frenzied flock of jays will surround the beleaguered raptor and harass it unmercifully until it finally leaves. Another favorite pastime is basking in the sun. On cool winter days, you might spot one in a sunny patch of lawn, breast facing the sun, raising its wings to expose its belly feathers to the warming rays. Or

it will lie breast down on the ground with its wings spread to warm its back and rump. Blue jays are equally enthusiastic bathers and give themselves with abandon to their daily ablutions in the bird bath or shallow pool. Lucky observers might even catch one excitedly rubbing ants over its feathers, a ritual of feather maintenance and surface bug-removal operation practiced by several songbirds.

Blue jays, while not highly gifted musicians, have a number of distinctive calls—a loud, harsh *jay* call uttered in three's, a distinctive rusty-gate note, and a curious gurgle yodel. They are also skilled mimics and reproduce a version of the red-shouldered hawk call that is almost impossible to distinguish from the real thing. In the spring, the female constructs a round bulky cup-nest made of twigs and bark strips five to twenty feet up in a tree. Nests are often garnished with plastic strips and string to lend an air of distinction. Males help with both nest construction and material supply. The female then lays four to five greenish buff eggs. Both male and female care for the young which fledge in seventeen to twenty days. While perhaps not a model of "perfect" behavior, blue jays will afford the observer hours of enjoyment as they congregate enthusiastically at your feeder.

CAROLINA CHICKADEE
Poecile carolinensis,
formerly *Parus carolinensis*

The delightful Carolina chickadee can be found throughout the eastern half of Texas.

Black-capped, black-bibbed, and decidedly cute, this agile gleaner of insects and snatcher of seeds is a delight to behold. Speaking its name to announce its presence, this mite of a bird is the southern look-alike of the black-capped chickadee. Carolina chickadees are fairly common through most of the eastern half of Texas south to the Nueces River. A frequent visitor to backyards, chickadees are mainly denizens of woodlands, edges of clearings, and brushy streamsides. They are especially attracted to tube-shaped feeders tailored to their small size which discourage larger, more aggressive seed-eating birds.

In the fall and winter, chickadees will band together with other small woodland birds such as the tufted titmouse, ruby-crowned kinglet, brown creeper, and downy woodpecker. These small mixed flocks comb the countryside in search of food, finding protection and better foraging opportunities by joining forces. Favorite food items include insects and their larvae and eggs, along with seeds and berries. There is perhaps nothing more mesmerizing than to watch a small group of chickadees flitting from branch to branch, working rapidly in a variety of positions, deftly nabbing morsels from the outer branch tips. You will rarely ever see a chickadee feed on the ground, but they will bathe periodically in your birdbath.

Male chickadees begin singing their four-note nuptial song, *fee-bee, fee-bay,* as early as late January and early February. Chickadees prefer to nest in deserted woodpecker holes or other tree cavities found in your yard or nearby woodland. They will also utilize nest boxes with appropriately-sized entrances. Females lay from five to eight white eggs lightly marked with reddish brown. Males and females take turns feeding the young, which leave the nest in thirteen to seventeen days. This small, plump, short-billed bird, at once tame and acrobatic, will provide you with loads of viewing pleasure as it makes quick trips to the feeder and back to its favorite perch in the nearby tree.

TUFTED TITMOUSE
Baeolophus bicolor, formerly *Parus bicolor*

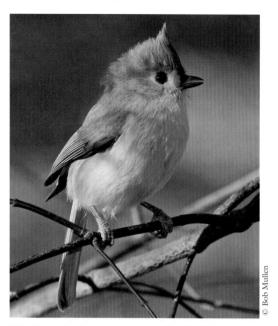

© Bob Mullen

The distinctive "peter! peter! peter!" call of the tufted titmouse can be heard in woodlands and suburban areas through most of Texas.

With a perky black crest and jaunty air, this small member of the tit family is all business and efficiency at the tube feeder. A quick learner and a problem solver, the smart little titmouse will be the first to learn how to negotiate a new feeder or find a way to retrieve a hard-to-reach morsel. Texas hosts two versions of the tufted titmouse, the gray crested form of the east and black crested form of the west. Tufted titmice are common to fairly common throughout most of the state. Bold and lively, the birds frequent oak groves and other woodland habitats. They can also be found along forest and prairie edges, in streamside thickets, and sparsely wooded pastures. They are common denizens of backyards in towns and cities as long as large trees and thick shrubbery are present.

Like the chickadees, titmice are important members of the wintering foraging flocks that roam the woodlands in search of food. The tufted titmouse has a bounding, quick, and slightly irregular flight as it pops from tree to tree, landing with a slight flourish of the tail. Unlike the Carolina chickadee, tufted titmice periodically descend to the ground to hunt for insects, their larvae, and eggs. They have a special yen for caterpillars and wasps, but will also snap up seeds, nuts, wild fruits, and berries when available.

Highly inquisitive and definitely not shy, they respond positively to whistles and *pishing* noises and will come immediately to investigate the situation. Their most common vocalization is the *peter, peter, peter* song. They also belt out a cardinal-like series of three to five notes all on the same pitch. Titmice have various scold notes, some of them sounding very chickadee-like, and they can produce all sorts of chortling sounds. During the nesting season these usually gregarious birds become aggressively territorial as they defend their nest site against potential intruders. As is the case for all cavity nesters, suitable snags are in high demand and very short supply. Like the Carolina chickadee, titmice will accept artificial nest boxes as long as the entrance is the proper size. An interesting facet of their nest construction behavior, titmice line the inside of the nest hole with all kinds of fur and animal hair and can sometimes be seen pulling the fur from live animals standing or sleeping nearby. Titmice maintain long-term pair bonds. Females lay from five to seven creamy white eggs which hatch in approximately fourteen days. Both males and females tend the nestlings, which fledge after fifteen to eighteen days. Interestingly, young of a previous brood will occasionally help at the nest.

CAROLINA WREN
Thryothorus ludovicianus

© TPWD

The Carolina wren is a versatile little bird which will nest in almost any available space.

Dressed in rich rufous with a golden ochre breast, the Carolina wren sings gloriously for its supper: an enticing array of insects, with caterpillars a special treat. Having a fondness for hanging baskets

of flowers, these close-sitting wrens will flush abruptly, often startling home gardeners who are merely watering their plants. For such a tiny bird, the Carolina wren belts out a resounding and insistent song: a clear *teakettle, teakettle, teakettle* or *cheery, cheery, cheery*. Its varied repertoire of scolds and calls keeps homeowners aware of nesting progress.

NORTHERN CARDINAL
Cardinalis cardinalis

© TPWD, Leroy Williamson

One of the brightest sights in winter is the crimson northern cardinal, seen here in its preferred brushy habitat.

With a cone-shaped reddish bill and conspicuous crest, the redbird and his tawny consort are favorites of the backyard garden. With a distinctive black patch at the base of its bill, the cardinal is the only all red-bodied bird in the United States that sports a crest. In Texas, cardinals occur throughout much of the state, though less regularly in the Trans-Pecos and western Panhandle. Highly adaptable to habitats altered by man, cardinals have continued to increase their range, especially northward. The proliferation of bird feeders may be partly responsible for this spread, as cardinals have an inordinate fondness for black oil sunflower seeds. In the more humid areas of Texas, cardinals frequent woodlands or open habitats with scattered trees, bushes, and an abundance of tall weeds. In the more arid regions to the west, cardinals tend to show up around vegetated stream-bottoms and residential areas landscaped with shade trees, shrubs, and water features. Preferring to forage on the ground, cardinals dine on a large variety of wildflowers and grass seeds. They will also eat wild fruits and berries, supplementing their diet with insects, snails, slugs, and mollusks, when available.

Strangely enough, both male and female cardinals will do heated battle with car mirrors and reflective windows, defending territory against their own reflections. Both males and females sing, though the male's nuptial song is more insistent and elaborate. Loud, clear, rich, and mellifluous, the song is a sustained series of variable, distinctively phrased whistles. The call note is a sharp and emphatic chip which is easy to recognize once you have heard it. Come nesting time you will notice the male providing tasty courtship feedings to his wing-fluttering mate. While the pair bond is maintained throughout the year, he becomes much more attentive and solicitous at this time. Indeed, until she lays her eggs, he hardly lets her out of his sight. Nests are placed from five to ten feet off the ground, usually in a well-hidden spot toward the center of a thick shrub. Once the female has laid the three to four eggs in the scantily-lined cup-shaped nest, the male will bring her tidbits of food as she incubates. He also performs a good many of the nest chores such as feeding the young and removing fecal sacs. Young fledge about twelve days after hatching. At this time the male will take over the feeding of the youngsters while the female starts a new brood.

HOUSE FINCH
Carpodacus mexicanus

Also known as the "Hollywood finch," the colorful and gregarious house finch is one of the earliest nesters of the season.

Otherwise known as the Hollywood finch, this gregarious cherry-colored finch with a brown cap and streaky belly sings a melodious song. Expanding its range to urban areas, it gives the ubiquitous house sparrow a good run for its money. House finches favor weed seeds but also flock to feeders where they plop themselves down to gorge on sunflower seeds, to the utter frustration of the titmice and chickadees who wait impatiently for the seed gluttons to leave.

CEDAR WAXWING
Bombycilla cedrorum

A dapper gentleman, the cedar waxwing is so named for its fondness of cedar and juniper berries, and for the drop of what looks like red sealing wax on its wings.

Always impeccably groomed, this sleek and elegant bird is an abundant wintertime visitor. The cedar waxwing's silky brown-buff plumage is set off smartly by a black mask, perky dark brown crest, short, yellow-tipped tail, and yellowish underparts. Waxwings get their curious name from the red waxlike spot found on the secondary wing feathers of most birds.

Cedar waxwings tend to be rather gypsylike in their occurrence. Arriving in mid-October or November, they can stay as late as May. They are irregularly abundant to fairly common throughout most of the state. Flying in tight formations, these highly gregarious birds often alight en masse in a fruiting tree. Watch for the "pass the berry" game, in which one bird passes an uneaten fruit to the next bird down the line to the end of the limb, the final bird gobbling it up with delight. Preferred habitats include dense to open woodlands, valleys, swamps, and tree-cloaked hills. They readily frequent cultivated areas bordering fields and private residences, especially those with ornamental fruiting trees. In the western regions, they gravitate toward the brushy and tree-lined stream bottoms. A major fruit lover, waxwings gorge on ripe cedar and juniper berries, hackberries, and pyracantha berries. A large flock can strip a tree of nearly all its fruit in a matter of minutes. When winters are marked by great fluctuations in temperature from long-term hard freezes to abrupt thaws and warm spells, wild fruits and berries will often become fermented. Large flocks of waxwings feasting on the tainted fruit can become hopelessly drunk. Birds then fall to the ground or wheel deliriously about crashing into cars, windows, or the paws of an onlooking cat. Cedar waxwings don't have elaborate songs. They emit high-pitched lisping calls, *see, see, see, see, see,* which do not carry over a long distance. Cedar waxwings are one of the major delights of the winter landscape, and along with American robins, brighten up those somber winter days.

RED-BELLIED WOODPECKER
Melanerpes carolinus

In the wild, red-bellied woodpeckers eat ants, beetles, berries, acorns, and corn. In backyards, the bird will partake of seeds, bread, fruit, suet, and even the sugar water set out for hummingbirds and orioles.

Also known as the "zebra" woodpecker, this noisy bird is the only bar-backed woodpecker with an entirely red crown. Favorite haunts in Texas include groves of deciduous trees, open stands of mixed coniferous forest, and stream and edge habitats in the eastern half of the state. Many Texans mistakenly call this bird with the red cap the red-headed woodpecker, and this is understandable because the so-

called red-belly is really a very pale coral, rarely visible in the field. The red-bellied woodpecker, also known as the "Chad" or "Chack" for one of his calls, is often heard before it is seen. A noisy bird, it also utters a soft, *churr* several times in succession.

Not a gregarious species, red-bellies are usually seen singly or in pairs. In settled areas, this woodpecker will often frequent backyards and orchards. It is one of the few members of the family that consumes more vegetable matter than insects. Berries, acorns, and corn are favorite food items. They also take ants and beetles and sometimes store them in cracks and tree crevices for a later day. Many suburban red-bellies are attracted to backyard feeders, partaking of seeds, bread, fruit, suet, and even sugar water set out for hummingbirds. A fairly common nester in large back yards or nearby woodlands with suitable snags, both male and female excavate the nest cavity. Birds will also use an artificial nest box, lining it with small bits of wood chips or sawdust. The female lays four to five elliptical white eggs that are sometimes glossy and sometimes matte finished. The male incubates the brood at night, with the female taking over for the day shift. Young fledge from twenty-four to twenty-seven days after hatching and will remain around the nest tree or nest box for the time it takes to learn how to forage for themselves.

DOWNY WOODPECKER
Picoides pubescens

The pint-sized downy woodpecker can often be seen feeding in mixed flocks with chickadees, titmice, and nuthatches.

Industrious and diligent, this smallest of our woodpeckers ranks as one of Texas' favorites. His cheerful *peek* call and his long, rattling, descending "whinny" resound from tree trunk and backyard suet feeders alike. This tame little bird hitches up a tree trunk headfirst by a series of hops and jumps, poking under a flake of bark here, looking into a crevice there, tapping attentively all the while in search of hidden insects. If you walk toward him as he pecks away at the trunk, he will merely circle coyly to the other side, then peer around to see if the coast is clear. He drills the trunk with his short awl of a bill and can often be seen dangling from twigs relieving the outer branches of any hapless insect or grub.

The downy ranges across North America, avoiding only the arid regions of the Desert Southwest. A year-round resident of eastern and northern Texas, he is one of the few of our woodpeckers whose range does not also extend into Mexico. Look for the downy feeding in mixed foraging flocks in open woodlots and parks in the company of chickadees, titmice, and nuthatches. Interestingly, downies go through a brief amorous stage in the fall. Heated rivalries, brief bouts of drumming and dancing soon give way, however, to renewed peaceful coexistence with the onset of cold weather. Birds excavate a new nest every year and often choose cottonwoods or other species found near water.

The downy lines the nest cavities with wood chips and dust and often camouflages it with surrounding moss, fungus, and lichens. The female lays four to five white eggs and both male and female incubate. After the eggs hatch the male is thought to do most of the brooding of the young. Young fledge approximately twenty-one days after hatching. Fledglings remain dependent upon their parents for their food and for learning how to forage until about three to four weeks after fledging.

© TPWD, Earl Nottingham

© TPWD

Feisty hummingbirds zipping about from flower to flower like so many glittering dive-bombers are a delight to watch, and you can easily attract them to almost any backyard. Their shining, jewel-like colors and fascinating behavior make hummingbirds among the most welcome visitors to the wildflower garden. Curious to the extreme and ever on the lookout for new sources of food, hummers will boldly explore your garden for suitable nectar sources.

In the wild, hummingbirds frequent meadows, lowland forest edges, and woodland openings. The key to creating an attractive habitat for these small creatures is to provide them with conditions that most closely approach those found in the wild. Floral variety, rich nectar sources, overlapping bloom times, running water, and adequate cover are prime ingredients.

Hummingbirds utilize two major sources of food: flower nectar and the tiny insects and spiders that are attracted to it. The sweet sap which exudes from holes that sapsuckers have made in trees is another food source. Hummers will also frequent special feeders, well placed for easy viewing, which contain sugar water of the proper concentration. While hummingbirds obtain most of their water from flower nectar, it is good to provide an additional source of running water for them to bathe in and drink. Even though hummers can use beads of water on a leaf or even the spray from a garden sprinkler, putting up a bird bath with a small mister, dripper, or waterfall is perhaps the most effective method of providing water for hummingbirds. Make sure the bird bath has areas of very shallow water so the birds are able to stand in the water if they choose to do so. Place a few flat rocks in the water to create various depths. Watching hummers absorbed in their daily bathing routine can be lots of fun for the whole family.

Hummingbirds mainly feed on flower nectar and the tiny insects and spiders that are attracted to it.

© TPWD, Frank Aguilar

Designing a Hummingbird Garden

Gardens designed to attract hummingbirds are easy to create. They can be as simple as a flower box of hummingbird plants arranged on a balcony or patio, or as elaborate and expansive as a formal parterre garden. Include native trees, shrubs, and vines along with native wildflowers. (See table 7.1 at the end of this chapter for a list of plants that hummingbirds favor.) Flowering shrubs are very effective hummingbird lures, as are trellises and fences covered with flowering vines. Rather than scattering flowers about, plant them in clusters. Incorporate areas of shade, partial sun, and full sun. Include tall trees, short, thick shrubbery, and low grassy areas to create a multi-tiered effect. The multilayered arrangement not only affords a wide choice of suitable foraging, perching, and resting areas, it also provides easy access to all the flowers. Hummers will make use of this extra space around the blooms to hover and forage comfortably.

Plants that Attract Hummingbirds

One of the most important steps in creating a hummingbird garden is selecting and planting appropriate flowers. While hummingbirds will visit nectar-bearing flowers of all colors, they are particularly drawn to bright red and orange tubular flowers. A garden rich in scarlet penstemon, red sages, and bright orange trumpet vine will catch the eye of any hummingbird passing nearby. However, you do not need to plant an all red flower garden to attract them. Once the birds discover suitably shaped flowers with abundant nectar, they will return to them. And, while hummingbirds are attracted to a variety of plants, native wildflowers and flowering shrubs are recommended.

Before selecting particular native plants, it is good to review some of the structural characteristics of the classic hummingbird flower. Many "hummingbird flowers" hang down in pendant fashion or are held horizontally in widely spaced clusters of flowers. This configuration gives the bird plenty of room to feed easily and lessens the possibility of entanglement. Most hummingbird flowers have tubular or trumpet-shaped blossoms with thick petal walls and

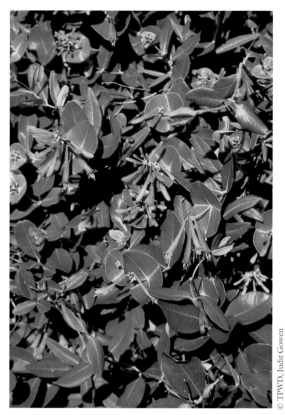

Coral honeysuckle is an ideal hummingbird plant, having orange-red tubular flowers that angle down, very tiny petals, very little scent, and copious nectar.

© TPWD, Judit Gowen

flexible stalks. Thick petal walls protect the delicate ovary at the base of the floral tube from the hummingbird's sharp bill, and also discourage cheaters, like carpenter bees, from nipping the base and stealing the nectar without pollinating the flower. Other blossoms have grooves which guide the cylindrical hummingbird bill to the nectar and away from fragile flower parts. Because hummingbirds have a very poor sense of smell, many hummingbird flowers save energy by not producing a fragrance.

Hummingbirds require a great deal of energy to maintain body temperature and sustain flight. For this reason, hummingbird flowers produce large amounts of nectar at frequent intervals. Unlike insects, hummingbirds do not require special floral platforms on which to land while feeding since the birds hover in the air in front of the flowers to drink the nectar.

The individual plants you select for the hummingbird garden will depend on which area in Texas you reside. Hummingbirds feed from a variety of different native plants. Ruby-throated hummingbirds, whose range extends throughout the eastern half of the United States, are especially attracted to red columbine, scarlet sage, coral honeysuckle, phlox, trumpet creeper, cross-vine, standing cypress, and various species of red, pink, and magenta penstemon. The black-chinned hummingbird, which summers throughout most of the western United States from central Texas to British Columbia, is attracted to ocotillo, tree tobacco, chuparosa, lantana, palo verde, butterfly bush, scarlet delphinium, paintbrushes, red columbine, agaves, scarlet gilia, various penstemons, and red yucca, to name a few. Many species of the hummingbirds that occur in the southwestern portion of the state include the blue-throated, broadtailed, magnificent, lucifer, rufous, and the occasional Anna's hummingbirds. The broad-billed, calliope, green violet-ear, violet-crowned, and white-eared hummingbirds also show up sporadically in our state. Native wildflowers and shrubs of the southwest such as paintbrush, penstemons, columbines, sky-rocket, agaves, lupines, red salvias, ocotillo, lobelia, and monkey-flowers are highly attractive to these species.

Hummingbird Feeders

It is easy to create a "fast food" hummingbird cafeteria by hanging one to several hummingbird feeders at various points around the outside of the house and in the yard. Position them for easy viewing from living room, bedroom, or kitchen windows so you can enjoy the show. If you are really enterprising, rig up a fluorescent spotlight to bring out the full iridescence of each species' body feathers as it comes to sip the nectar. It is important to purchase or construct the nectar-containing feeder in order to discourage ants and bees who will also be attracted to the sugary solution. You might also try to block pesky ants and bees from the feeder by applying Vaseline to the pole or the wire holding the feeder. Some feeders have specially designed bee guards that fit over the feeder holes making it difficult for bees to reach the fluid. Other feeders have even been designed with an "ant moat," a tiny bowl of water fitted around the feeder hanging wire that prevents the ants or other crawling insects from traveling down the wire to the feeding ports of the feeder.

Bottles or feeders hung among the blossoms of flowering shrubs are speedily discovered by

It's easy to make the sugar-water nectar hummingbirds eagerly lap up: Just combine four parts water with one part granulated white sugar, boil, cool, and fill the feeder.

hummingbirds. Hummingbirds are sometimes so bold that you may be able to attract one by simply holding a bright red flower in your hand while standing a short distance from a flowering shrub. Sitting quietly in a lawn chair wearing a red T-shirt or bright red cap may also arouse the curiosity of one of these feisty creatures.

After you purchase or construct your hummingbird feeder, you need to fill it with hummingbird food. There are commercial solutions available on the market which you can purchase, but it is just as simple to make your own at home. A good recipe for a homemade mixture is one part sugar to four parts water, which closely approximates the ratio of sugar to water in the nectar of many hummingbird flowers. White granulated sugar is best to use. Boil the mixture for one to two minutes and then let it cool. This process will help to delay fermentation. Do not use honey since it harbors a fungus that could be a health threat to the birds.

Fill the feeder and store the remaining liquid in the refrigerator. It is not necessary to add red food dye to the solution. Many feeders on the market are made of red plastic or have red somewhere on the plastic covering. This will be more than enough

color to attract the birds. Make sure that you clean the hummingbird feeder every few days, as hummingbird liquid is highly susceptible to mold and bacteria, which may present a health hazard to the birds, especially in hot weather. Cleanse feeder bottles and nectar ports with soap and water, or a combination of baking soda and vinegar (watch out: this combination fizzes). Rinse feeders thoroughly to remove all residue. You will find that some designs of hummingbird feeders are easier to clean than others.

Since most species of hummingbirds are migratory, feeders should be set in place to coincide with the birds' arrival in the spring. The arrival date, of course, will depend on which part of Texas you live in and on the migratory patterns of the birds. Your local Audubon Society will have inexpensive bird check lists available for your region which will indicate average spring arrival and fall departure times of hummingbirds for your part of the state. To find your local Audubon Society chapter, call the National Audubon Society office in Texas at 512-306-8751. In addition, refer to any of several field guides to the North American birds. These sources will inform you about when you can expect to see hummingbirds and which species of hummingbirds to look for in your area.

It is a misconception that it is harmful to leave a feeder up too late in the fall. Doing this will not prevent a hummingbird from migrating. Feeders that are left up longer than usual may actually help late migrating hummers, since they will provide the birds with the critical extra energy they need to complete

It is almost impossible to differentiate between the species of some female hummingbirds. This little female is either a ruby-throated or black-chinned hummingbird.

the journey in an environment that may be devoid of flowering nectar plants. If you choose to leave your feeders up only during migration periods, though, a good rule of thumb is to wait until one week after you see the last hummingbird before you remove your feeders.

Placement of feeders is very important. If possible, try to hang feeders in the shade and out of the wind. It is a good idea initially to place feeders near native wildflowers that are naturally attractive to hummingbirds. This may speed up the discovery process. It is better to have already created a habitat garden where hummingbirds are likely to visit before hanging up the feeders. The addition of feeders to the garden will simply increase the traffic by offering more foraging opportunities to more individuals.

Don't be disturbed to find out that hummers can be very aggressive and sometimes outright belligerent with one another when it comes to sharing a feeder. Chases abound and they may expend a good deal of energy in establishing a dominant position around well-placed feeders. It is always interesting to observe the hummers as they jostle for position in the pecking order. You will soon get to recognize which bird is the alpha individual, so to speak. To minimize spats, place feeders far apart in locations out of view from one another.

While most feeders are quickly attended by a host of hungry hummers, there are a few reasons a feeder may seem to go unused.

WHEN HUMMERS WON'T COME TO A FEEDER

It can be frustrating to put up hummingbird feeders if birds don't appear. The reasons hummingbirds may not discover the feeders are numerous and complex. A few possible reasons for an absence of hummers are:

⌦ Lack of patience. It may take a few weeks for hummingbirds to find feeders. Once discovered, however, they will return year after year. Be sure to keep the solution fresh and clean, even if you don't think the birds are around.

⌦ The feeding solution level may be too low or may be fermented. This is often the case in a climate like Texas where the heat of only two or three afternoons can ferment the solution. If you have left your feeder empty for too long a period, hummers will go find food elsewhere.

⌦ Sometimes it only appears that hummers are not using the feeder. Much of their time is spent perching and preening inconspicuously in a nearby tree. Hummers may then zip to the feeder when you are not looking.

⌦ Hummingbirds will often use the feeders heavily during migration periods, but when it comes time for the females to build their nest, they will become much more secretive and inconspicuous. Again, be patient. Come the end of August, little migrants will be back looking for food to fuel their upcoming voyage to the tropics.

Black-chinned hummingbirds are found throughout the western half of Texas.

Some species of sphinx moths, also called "hummingbird moths," mimic hummingbirds. Their wings hum like the hummingbird's, the proboscis (part of an insects mouthparts) extends out to resemble the hummingbird's beak, and they hover just like hummingbirds. Sphinx moths are also important pollinators.

☞ There may be so much food in the wild that hummers do not need to supplement their diet. If given a choice, hummers prefer flowering plants and shrubs. When bloom periods are over, however, they will return faithfully to the well-supplied feeders.

☞ If your neighborhood does not have an abundance of wildflowers, hummingbirds may just not be attracted to that area. Neighborhoods with lots of nectar-rich flowers are a mecca for hummers.

☞ There may be too many aggressive bees and ants around your feeder which make foraging difficult and dangerous for the hummers. Try installing bee guards and ant moats (available at almost any shop that carries birdfeeders), or greasing the post or hanging wire. For the hummingbirds' protection, be sure to keep insecticides and other foreign substances away from the feeder ports.

Hosting hummers in your backyard will require work and planning, but once your hummer habitat is established and the birds have discovered it, they will repay you with hours of enjoyment. Their beauty more than makes up for the labor involved.

The only hummingbird found in the eastern part of Texas and the United States is the colorful ruby-throated hummingbird.

RUBY-THROATED HUMMINGBIRD
Archilocus colubris

The darting flight and insistent squeaks and chitters of a hummingbird are sure signs that spring has arrived. The male ruby-throated hummingbird is a tiny bird, sporting a bright red throat patch, or gorget, and a beautiful bronze-green back. Females are a little less fancy, with a white-gray throat and underparts, white spots on the outside tips of the tail, and the same beautiful bronze-green back. Neither male nor female weighs much more than a penny, and they are both lively additions to any rural, suburban, or urban garden.

The little ruby-throat migrates from Central America to the eastern half of the United States as well as southern Canada in the spring to breed. Many of the hummingbirds will migrate directly over the Gulf of Mexico, making a 650-mile nonstop flight on the energy of just a few grams of fat. Females construct their tiny nests primarily out of plant bud scales held together with spider silk, lined with plant down, and decorated with bits of lichen. Her two eggs resemble navy beans in size, shape, and color. In the fall and after the nesting period, the ruby-throat migrates again south to the wintering grounds of Central America. Since ruby-throated hummingbirds are very curious, providing feeders and flowers, especially red or orange flowers, in your garden is almost always rewarded with a visit from the little birds.

The beautiful male black-chinned hummingbird sports a black chin and a blue-purple "collar."

BLACK-CHINNED HUMMINGBIRD
Archilochus alexandri

Breeding from Texas, where it is the most common hummingbird, all the way up into British Columbia, the black-chinned hummingbird has the most extensive breeding range of any western hummingbird. As its name suggests, the black-chin is the only North American hummingbird to feature a black throat patch edged by a glittering band of amethyst-purple iridescence. Metallic green above with dull green sides and flanks and whitish underparts, black-chins closely resemble their eastern counterpart, the ruby-throated hummingbird—especially in poor light. When the telltale gorget is not visible, male black-chins can sometimes be distinguished by their slightly darker underparts and narrow white collar. Females of the two species, however, are almost impossible to distinguish in the field.

Over much of the west, this hummer is widespread in a variety of semi-arid habitats at lower elevations. It often frequents suburban gardens and will sometimes nest in backyards within its range. In addition to well-flowered residential areas, preferred habitats include semi-dry brush country, chaparral, and river groves. In Texas, black-chins are known to nest across the central and western counties, as far east as San Antonio, Austin, and Dallas.

The black-chin's feeding habits are similar to those of the ruby-throat, perhaps with a greater tendency to watch for small flying insects from a conspicuous perch, sallying out after them in the manner of a flycatcher. One of the more vocal hummingbirds, black-chins utter a cascade of high-pitched squeals and twittering notes. Some writers have compared its high-pitched song to a person whistling through his or her teeth. Call notes consist of a soft *tchew*, but when squabbling with others at a well-defended feeder, chip notes are spewed out in rapid-fire succession.

Males attract females by performing elaborate aerial courtship displays consisting of a series of deep looping dives and elaborate figure eights. After mating, the female assumes all nesting duties while the male seeks to impress other potential mates. Females build a tiny, walnut-sized nest of plant down and spider webs much like that of the ruby-throat except that they do not use lichens so extensively for adornment. The female alone incubates the two pea-sized white eggs until they hatch about sixteen days later. She feeds the tiny, helpless chicks a rich diet of nectar, insects, and spiders which she administers by regurgitation, inserting her bill deep into their throats. Chicks accept the food in the manner of a mini sword swallower, a disconcerting sight for almost anyone who first witnesses the process. Within two weeks, the chicks begin exercising their wings and are soon to fledge—two more incredible feathered flying machines set out into the world.

Table 7.1
PLANTS FAVORED BY HUMMINGBIRDS

* Not native to Texas, but not invasive. ** Considered naturalized.
Note: Plants are listed alphabetically by family. Numbered regions correspond to the Texas Ecoregion map on page 10.

Common Name	Scientific Name	1	2	3	4	5	6	7	8	9	10
Acanthus Family	**Acanthaceae**										
Flame Acanthus	*Anisacanthus quadrifidus* var. *wrightii*							X			
Hummingbird Plant	*Anisacanthus puberulus*										X
Shrimp Plant	*Justicia brandegeena**						X				
Agave Family	**Agavaceae**										
Century Plant	*Agave americana*		X				X			X	
Century Plant	*Agave perryi* ssp. *neomexicana*										X
Red-flowered Yucca	*Hesperaloe parviflora*			X	X	X		X			
Catalpa Family	**Bignoniaceae**										
Cross-vine	*Bignonia capreolata*	X	X	X	X						
Trumpet-creeper	*Campsis radicans*	X	X	X	X	X	X	X			
Desert Willow	*Chilopsis linearis*						X	X			X
Yellow Trumpets	*Tecoma stans*							X			X
Borage Family	**Boraginaceae**										
Geiger Tree	*Cordia sebestena**						X				
Pineapple Family	**Bromeliaceae**										
Air Pine	*Tillandsia baileyi*						X				
Cactus Family	**Cactaceae**										
Hedgehog Cactus	*Echinocereus triglochidiatus*						X		X	X	X
Bluebell Family	**Campanulaceae**										
Cardinal Flower	*Lobelia cardinalis*	X	X	X	X	X	X	X	X	X	X
Honeysuckle Family	**Caprifoliaceae**										
Coral Honeysuckle	*Lonicera sempervirens*	X	X	X	X	X					
Pink Family	**Caryophyllaceae**										
Western Catchfly	*Silene laciniata*										X
Catchfly	*Silene subciliata*	X	X	X							

Common Name	Scientific Name	1	2	3	4	5	6	7	8	9	10
Morning Glory Family	**Convolvulaceae**										
Red Morning Glory	Ipomoea coccinea*	x	x								
Scarlet Morning Glory	Ipomoea cristulata										x
Cypress Vine	Ipomoea quamoclit*	x	x								
Heath Family	**Ericaceae**										
Hoary Azalea	Rhododendron canescens	x									
Texas White Azalea	Rhododendron oblongifolium	x									
Ocotillo Family	**Fouquieriaceae**										
Ocotillo	Fouquieria splendens										x
Horsechestnut Family	**Hippocastanaceae**										
White Buckeye	Aesculus glabra v. arguta	x		x	x	x		x			
Red Buckeye	Aesculus pavia	x	x	x	x			x	x		
Mint Family	**Lamiaceae**										
Prairie Brazoria	Warnockia scutellarioides			x	x	x		x			
Purple Horsemint	Monarda citriodora	x	x	x	x	x	x	x	x	x	x
Wild Bergamot	Monarda fistulosa	x	x	x	x						
Spotted Beebalm	Monarda punctata	x	x	x	x	x		x	x		
Tropical Sage	Salvia coccinia	x	x	x	x	x	x	x			
Autumn Sage	Salvia greggii				x		x	x			x
Crimson Sage	Salvia henryi										x
Big Red Sage	Salvia penstemonoides			x	x	x		x			
Cedar Sage	Salvia roemeriana							x			x
Mountain Sage	Salvia regla										x
Red Hedge-nettle	Stachys coccinia	x	x								
Legume Family	**Fabaceae**										
Lead-plant Amorpha	Amorpha canescens	x	x	x	x	x		x	x		
False Indigo	Amorpha fruticosa	x	x	x	x	x	x	x			
Smooth Amorpha	Amorpha laevigata	x	x								
Panicled Amorpha	Amorpha paniculata	x									

Table 7.1 cont.
PLANTS FAVORED BY HUMMINGBIRDS

* Not native to Texas, but not invasive. ** Considered naturalized.
Note: Plants are listed alphabetically by family. Numbered regions correspond to the Texas Ecoregion map on page 10.

Common Name	Scientific Name	1	2	3	4	5	6	7	8	9	10
Legume Family continued											
Anacacho Orchid-tree	*Bauhinia lunarioides*			x	x	x		x			
Bird of Paradise	*Caesalpinia gilliesii**							x			x
False Mesquite	*Calliandra conferta*						x	x			x
Fairy Duster	*Calliandra eriophylla**						x	x			x
Eastern Coral Bean	*Erythrina herbacea*		x	x	x	x					
Scarlet Runner Bean	*Phaseolus coccineus**	x	x	x	x	x	x	x			
Bristly Locust	*Robinia hispida*	x									
New Mexico Locust	*Robinia neomexicana*										x
Rattlebush	*Sesbania drummondii*		x	x	x	x	x	x			
Showy Sesbania	*Sesbania punicea**	x									
Logania Family	**Loganaceae**										
Carolina Jessamine	*Gelsemium sempervirens*	x	x	x							
Pink-root	*Spigelia marilandica*	x		x							
Magnolia Family	**Magnoliaceae**										
Tulip Tree	*Liriodendron tulipifera*	x									
Mallow Family	**Malvaceae**										
Heart-leaf Hibiscus	*Hibiscus martianus*		x				x	x			
Scarlet Hibiscus	*Hibiscus coccineus*	x									
Turk's Cap	*Malvaviscus arboreus*	x	x	x	x	x	x	x			
Globe-mallow	*Sphaeralcea angustifolia*					x		x	x	x	x
Four-o'clock Family	**Nyctaginaceae**										
Hierba de la Hormiga	*Allionia incarnata*									x	x
Colorado Four-o'-clock	*Mirabilis multiflora*										x
Scarlet Four-o'-clock	*Mirabilis coccinea*										x
Scarlet Muskflower	*Nyctaginia capitata*		x	x	x	x		x	x	x	x
Phlox Family	**Polemoniaceae**										
Scarlet Standing Cypress	*Ipomopsis aggregata*										x
Standing Cypress	*Ipomopsis rubra*	x		x	x	x	x	x			

Common Name	Scientific Name	Region									
		1	2	3	4	5	6	7	8	9	10
Phlox Family	**Polemoniaceae**										
Drummond's Phlox	*Phlox drummondii*	X	X	X	X	X	X	X			
Polemonium	*Polemonium pauciflorum*										X
Buttercup Family	**Ranunculaceae**										
Texas Clematis	*Clematis texensis*			X	X	X		X			
Wild Columbine	*Aquilegia canadensis*	X		X	X	X		X			
Soapberry Family	**Sapindaceae**										
Mexican Buckeye	*Ungnadia speciosa*	X	X	X	X	X		X			X
Rose Family	**Rosaceae**										
Prairie Rose	*Rosa setigera*	X		X	X	X					
Madder Family	**Rubiaceae**										
Trompetilla	*Bouvardia ternifolia*										X
Orange Hamelia	*Hamelia patens**						X				
Figwort Family	**Scrophulariaceae**										
Texas Paintbrush	*Castilleja indivisa*	X	X	X	X	X	X				
Grassland Paintbrush	*Castilleja integra*										X
Woolly Paintbrush	*Castilleja lanata*										X
Cenizo	*Leucophyllum frutescens*						X	X			X
Snapdragon Vine	*Maurandella antirrhiniflora*	X	X	X	X	X	X	X			X
Havards' Penstemon	*Penstemon havardii*										X
Cup-leaf Penstemon	*Penstemon murrayanus*	X	X	X							
Three-flower Penstemon	*Penstemon triflorus*							X			
Wright's Penstemon	*Penstemon wrightii*										X
Nightshade Family	**Solanaceae**										
Shrubby Tobacco	*Nicotiana glauca***			X	X	X	X	X			X
Verbena Family	**Verbenaceae**										
Lantana	*Lantana urticoides*	X	X	X	X	X	X	X	X		X

© TPWD

© TPWD, Jim Whitcomb

A surprising number of Texas mammals will show up in backyard settings given the appropriate conditions. Deer, jackrabbits, cottontail rabbits, shrews, fox and gray squirrels, armadillos, foxes, raccoons, opossums, moles, and bats are some of the mammals you may observe in a well-rounded backyard habitat. Cute and furry, backyard mammals are generally more shy and skittish than their avian neighbors. Often, evidence of their dens and food caches (collections) can be found in sheltered areas under decks, piled debris, dog houses, in large clumps of grass and fallen logs, or in burrows dug beneath the ground, under large tree roots, and excavated high up in trees.

While it is more difficult to observe mammals because of their secretive and often nocturnal habits, with a little extra effort and by knowing where and when to look, you can often catch glimpses of their activities.

Texas also hosts an exceedingly rich array of native herptiles or "herps," for short. Indeed, the Lone Star state boasts approximately 70 species of amphibians and 165 species of reptiles. Most of them are small, secretive, and need a little bit of "wildness" in which to hide and find food. If you are lucky enough to live near a stream or pond close to woods, you could observe various salamanders, frogs, turtles, lizards, and snakes in your backyard or wildflower garden.

Mammals

If you live in an urban area, you shouldn't expect to attract larger mammals such as mountain lions or bobcats. However, if you happen to live within their range in isolated wilderness areas, or have extensive stands of suitable habitat adjoining your neighborhood, these animals may pass within viewing range.

To attract small mammals to your yard, provide special areas of cover to protect them from predators. Brush piles are especially good means of providing a habitat structure for cottontail rabbits and squirrels, especially if vegetative cover is scarce. It is also important to give special protection to cavity trees on your land. Nest boxes can substitute for natural cavities if your property is snag-poor. Protect nearby streams, marshes, and swamps from water pollution and degradation. Create extensive edge areas with maximum habitat diversity. Plant native trees, shrubs, and vines with edible fruits and nuts, such as oaks, pines, junipers, wild cherries, mulberries, and wax myrtles. Provide sufficient areas of low cover to serve as protective shelter from dogs and cats, as well as from adverse weather. Erect special bat houses to attract Mexican free-tailed bats.

EASTERN FOX SQUIRREL
Sciurus niger

Fox squirrels prefer to nest in hollow trees, but will also inhabit large, leafy, and globe-shaped nests high up in trees.

Either you love the fox squirrel or you hate him. This little fellow is undeniably cute, but tends not to endear himself to those who love to feed wild birds. As any bird watcher can tell you, the fox squirrel is almost impossible to deter from bird feeders. Inquisitive and intelligent, the fox squirrel is adept at learning how to manipulate devices such as bird feeders in order to obtain food.

The fox squirrel is a large tree squirrel with rusty or reddish underparts and brownish or grayish upperparts. The tail is fluffy, less than half of its body length, and is colored with a mix of cinnamon, black, and cream. Fox squirrels dwell in most of the eastern two-thirds of Texas, and are very commonly seen in open woodlands as well as suburban areas. Folks often spot the large, leafy, globe-shaped nests the squirrels build high up in trees; however, they prefer hollow trees as nesting and denning sites. Acorns constitute the majority of their diet, but the squirrels also eat a variety of nuts, insects, green shoots, fruits, seeds, and buds. Females give birth to an average of four naked, blind, and helpless young per year. The young develop slowly, beginning to venture out of the nest at about seven to eight weeks. At ten to eleven months, the young are fully mature. Their frenzied chasing and boisterous barking are often the first happy signs to us that the young have left the nest and have ventured out on their own.

RINGTAIL
Bassariscus astutus

While it looks like a cross between a raccoon and a domestic cat, the ringtail is a species in its own right. It occurs throughout Texas and is cousin to the raccoon.

Some people falsely profess that the ringtail is a cross between a domestic cat and a raccoon. While closely related to the raccoon, the ringtail is its own species and is an exceptionally attractive cat-sized carnivore easily identified by its long, bushy, black and white ringed tail and slim body. Although the ringtail is rarely seen, it can be found throughout Texas, preferring rocky areas such as rock piles, stone fences, and canyon walls. Ringtails will also occupy hollow trees and logs, and are exceptional climbers. The ringtail is primarily active at night, and will spend most of the day in its den. Like its wily cousin, the raccoon, the ringtail will eat a variety of foods, including small birds, mammals, "herps" such as snakes, lizards, toads and frogs, crickets and grasshoppers, spiders, scorpions, and centipedes, and fruits of native plants, such as persimmon, hackberry, and mistletoe. California gold miners of the late 1940s thought the ringtail was an admirable substitute for their mousing domestic cats back home and would often encourage them to take up residence near their homes to make nightly "mouse hunts."

BATS

Texas records the largest number of bat species in the nation: thirty-two out of a possible forty-one species. While most bats live in caves, tree foliage, and bark, some species will take up residence in mines, tunnels, bridges, old buildings, and bat houses. Most bats in the United States weigh less than one ounce, but they may appear larger due to the size of their wings.

In the United States, all but three species of bats primarily feed on a variety of insects and arthropods, including moths, crickets, mosquitoes, and scorpions. These prey items are hunted both in the air and on the ground. Bats are particularly important in the United States for their contribution in the control of night-flying insects. According to Bat Conservation International, many bats consume 2,000 or more insects in just one night, and some can gobble up 600 mosquitoes in just one hour. Many of the insects that bats devour are considered agricultural pests such as the corn borer and cutworm moths. For this reason, large colonies of bats are extremely important for insect control. A flourishing bat population is a good alternative to chemical insect control, which is a threat to both personal and environmental health.

People have been putting up bat houses for over sixty years. Providing artificial roosts for the winged mammal is becoming increasingly important to their survival as their traditional roosts in old trees and

In Texas, most species of bats are very beneficial, feeding on a variety of insects and arachnids including moths, beetles, mosquitoes, crickets, and scorpions.

buildings are becoming more and more scarce. Bat houses are commercially available in nature stores, or you can find plans to build one in woodworking books or at Bat Conservation International's Web Site (www.batcon.org).

MEXICAN FREE-TAILED BAT
Tadarida brasiliensis

Mexican free-tailed bats are extremely beneficial mammals: each bat consumes up to 2000 insects each night!

Squeaking and swooping in the evening, Mexican free-tailed bats are the most common of our bats in Texas. The half-ounce free-tailed bat is medium-sized with dark brown or dark gray fur. It is also a member of a family of bats known as Molossidae, or free-tailed bats, which are so named because their tails extend beyond the uropatagium, the thin membrane that spans the two hind legs like the webbing between the toes of ducks.

Mexican free-tailed bats typically inhabit caves or unoccupied parts of buildings, crevices in large rocks, or nooks in structures such as buildings, bridges, and signs. These bats are also migratory and during migration, may stop over to roost in old cliff swallow nests. Bat excrement, known as "guano," has been harvested since the nineteenth century for use as fertilizer and fuel. The Mexican free-tail represents a very real threat to insects: they feast nightly on the swarms of the pesky critters. They have been found to prey on moths, flying ants, June beetles and leaf beetles, leafhoppers, and other bugs, and are estimated to consume from 6,000 to 18,000 metric tons of insects annually in Texas.

Texas is home to a variety of lizards such as geckos, skinks, iguanids, glass and alligator lizards, as well as whiptail lizards. This little prairie lizard is found in a variety of habitats of central and western Texas.

Reptiles and Amphibians

While many people think of reptiles and amphibians as slimy, slithery, creepy, or scary critters, they are really fascinating animals in their own right. Moreover, they perform an important ecological service for us by preying on noxious insects and rodents. If the idea of attracting these wonderful creatures appeals to you, there are a few things you can do to make your yard attractive to them.

LURING REPTILES AND AMPHIBIANS TO YOUR YARD

✍ Leave stones, stumps, and rotting logs in place. They can be creatively and attractively incorporated into almost any garden and provide valuable shelter and food resources for a variety of herps.

One key to providing habitat for many reptiles and amphibians is to provide easily accessible water and moist soil areas.

🖎 Create brush piles and wood piles at the edge of your yard to provide valuable shelters and basking sites for these cold-blooded creatures.

🖎 For borders around flower beds and ponds, consider constructing a wall of loose stones instead of using mortar. The crevices, nooks, and crannies will be home and hideout to a variety of amphibians and lizards.

🖎 Reduce lawn area. Reptiles and amphibians prefer native ground covers, grasses, and wildflowers to a finely manicured carpet of St. Augustine grass.

🖎 Keep your cat indoors. Cats, both domestic and feral, are serious predators of amphibians and reptiles. Poikilotherms (cold-blooded animals) are often sluggish, especially on cooler days, and are no match for the speed and stealth of these efficient hunters.

🖎 When possible, avoid the use of pesticides and lawn chemicals. Amphibians and their prey are especially sensitive to these chemicals.

🖎 Allow leaf litter, which is coveted habitat for many herps, to accumulate in flower beds or odd corners of a yard.

🖎 Provide easily accessible water and moist soil areas.

🖎 Well-aerated, friable soils (ones that crumble easily) are best for burrowing herptiles.

REPTILES

Texas hosts 165 species of reptiles, including 1 crocodilian, 35 turtles, 61 lizards, and 68 snakes. Turtles are highly distinctive with their peculiar bony shells and skeletons, scaly skin, toothless heads, and wide variety of pattern and color. All turtles have shells. The upper shell (carapace) and a lower shell (plastron) are connected at the sides by bony bridges. All turtles lay eggs which are deposited in a shallow nest which the female has constructed out of damp soil.

Sixty-one lizards call Texas home, among them are the geckos, skinks, iguanids, glass and alligator lizards, and whiptail lizards. Lizards are highly variable in color, pattern and size. They all have scaly skin, most have external ear openings (except for the earless lizards) and claws on their toes (except for the glass lizard, which has no legs). Lizards can be found in a variety of habitats, and while the majority lay eggs, some bear live young. Most lizards are diurnal, remaining active throughout the day.

The sixty-eight species of Texas snakes include blind snakes, colubrid snakes (the large majority of Texas snakes), elapid snakes (coral snakes), and vipers (rattlesnakes, copperheads, and cottonmouths). Snakes are thought by some herpetologists to be the most successful of all living reptiles, ranging farther north and to higher altitudes and adapting to a wider range of habitats than crocodiles, turtles, or lizards. Snakes are specialized for capturing particular kinds of prey such as earthworms, snails, slugs, amphibians, and small reptiles. Of the 113 species and subspecies of snakes, less than 15% are venomous. Indeed, the majority are totally harmless. Snakes fill very special roles in our ecosystem by controlling rodent and other pest species populations.

RED-EARED SLIDER
Trachemys scripta elegans

The red-eared slider is perhaps the best known and most recognizable of turtles. The top of the shell is smooth and gently curved and is olive to black with yellow stripes and bars. It is a medium-sized turtle, best identified by the red or sometimes yellow patch found just behind its eye. It is at home

The red-eared slider is almost exclusively aquatic, but is often seen basking on logs, exposed rocks, or vegetation.

in quiet, freshwater systems that have muddy bottoms and abundant aquatic vegetation. They range from Indiana to New Mexico down through Texas to the Gulf of Mexico. They are widely distributed throughout Texas except the far western region.

The red-eared slider is almost exclusively aquatic, and only rarely ventures out of water to lay its eggs or to migrate to a new body of water. Young turtles generally eat insect larvae and small fish, but as they age, their favorite food gradually switches to vegetation. The slider is commonly seen basking in the sun on logs, exposed rocks, or atop masses of vegetation. When basking sites are in short supply, they may even pile on top of each other up to three turtles deep.

Red-eared sliders may produce up to three clutches of four to twenty-three eggs in a single year. The female constructs each nest on the shore by digging a shallow depression, three to ten inches wide. She deposits her eggs in these excavations and subsequently covers them up. Although the young turtles may spend the winter in the nest, they generally hatch sixty to seventy-five days after being laid.

ORNATE BOX TURTLE
Terrapene ornata ornata

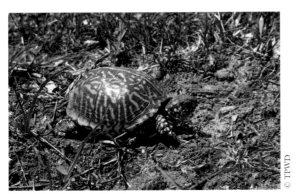

The ornate box turtle is an extravagantly marked reptile found throughout most of Texas. It dines on insects, berries, and carrion.

This beautifully marked diurnal turtle spends most of its time on the land. With a dome-shaped, elegantly-patterned carapace, squared off snout, hooked beak, and front legs sporting large orange spots, the ornate box turtle is certainly an attractive reptile. When alarmed, it closes its shell tightly at both ends in defense. It prefers sandy soils in semi-arid regions

on grasslands, plains, and in tame pastures throughout most of Texas, except for the extreme western portion of the Trans-Pecos. Males are distinguished from females by eye color; males have red eyes while the eyes of females are yellow. This interesting turtle dines on a variety of insects, with a special taste for dung-beetles, as well as berries and carrion. Females lay two to eight eggs in a shallow, flask-shaped nest she digs in sandy soils any time from May to July.

GREEN ANOLE
Anolis carolinensis

Commonly incorrectly called a chameleon, the green anole will change its color in response to a variety of situations, including light quality, temperature, and emotion.

Another common inhabitant of backyard gardens is the elegant green anole, sometimes incorrectly called the chameleon for its ability to change color from green to brown. Color change can be triggered by a number of factors including light quality, temperature, and emotion. Often seen during breeding season rhythmically extending its flashy rose to orange dewlap (fold of skin under its neck), combative males both attract mates and establish territories which they defend vigorously against all rivals. This arboreal lizard is common throughout the eastern half of Texas with a separate population occurring in extreme South Texas along the Rio Grande. It is active during the day, climbing high into trees, shrubs, and vines, and also on fences and walls in the garden. Very sensitive to low moisture levels, this attractive lizard requires shade, shelter, and a moist environment to survive the long hot Texas summers.

TEXAS RAT SNAKE
Elaphe obsoleta

The nonvenomous Texas rat snake is the serpent most often found up in the rafters of barns, lofts, and attics in rural and suburban areas.

A powerful constrictor, the Texas rat snake is a feisty, long, bluish black and olive brown blotched serpent ranging from forty-two to seventy-two inches long. Its background color is gray or yellowish and the head is usually black. Sometimes there may be a hint of red on the skin between the scales. The underside of the tail tip is commonly solid gray. This species exhibits considerable individual variation in pattern and coloration within its range in Texas. Adults are fairly unmistakable, but juveniles may resemble other rat snakes like the Great Plains rat snake and Baird's rat snake. It is also similar to the prairie kingsnake and the bullsnake.

In Texas, this snake is commonly found in rural and suburban areas from the central through the eastern half of Texas in a wide variety of habitats including pine forests, deciduous woodlands, pasturelands, stream valleys, and rocky canyons. In suburban areas, they tend to hide out in barn rafters, lofts, attics, or abandoned machinery and automobiles. The Texas rat snake prefers to prey on birds, their nestlings and eggs, as well as rodents, other small mammals, and lizards. The Texas rat snake is a highly agile climber, making its way up and down trunks of large trees with relative ease, thanks to high-traction belly scales.

It is also an accomplished swimmer and is often found patrolling river banks from the water.

The Texas rat snake is not venomous; however, it does tend to have an aggressive temperament. When threatened, it will rear its head, hiss, simulate a rattle by vibrating its tail in dry grass, and sometimes strike at the offender. The bite rarely succeeds in inflicting serious injury since the pressure of its jaws is insufficient to cause major damage.

Hawks are one of the main predators of the Texas rat snake, though it is also preyed upon by various mammals and other snakes. Hawks can easily locate the rat snake since it is often the subject of noisy mobbing activity by small birds when the snake is in the process of raiding a bird's nest.

CHECKERED GARTER SNAKE
Thamnophis marcianus marcianus

The elegant checkered garter snake is found through north, central, and the southern coastal plains of Texas.

The checkered garter snake is a brown, olive, or tan snake with a bold checkered pattern of large, squarish black spots over its body that diminishes toward the tail. Uppermost spots impinge upon the creamy yellow central back stripe, and side stripes are also light in color. The best field mark is a pale yellowish crescent moon shape just behind a large black spot on the side of the neck. The belly is yellow with no pattern. Most grow about two feet long and look very similar to the Western plains garter snake, superficially like the Texas and blackneck garter snakes, and somewhat like the ribbon snakes.

The checkered garter snake occurs throughout the western two-thirds of the state and is also commonly found in much of the southern part of the state. This species is seen most often during late spring and early summer in Texas. They can be found in grassy upland areas near water in north and central Texas but are more common in thorn scrub and brushy habitats on the lower coastal plain. This species seldom appears to stray far from permanent water.

This moderately slender terrestrial snake preys on earthworms, toads, frogs, fishes, and sometimes small rodents. Most commonly seen on warm, humid nights, they tend to forage at dawn and dusk in the fall and spring, but are predominantly nocturnal during the hot summer months. Warm evening showers apparently encourage food-seeking activities. This species will often take refuge in burrows or rock crevices, as well as under logs, rocks, and piles of debris.

The checkered garter snake is not venomous, but may nip if handled in a rough manner. When picked up, they will release a foul-smelling splash of feces from their vent and anal glands. Coyotes, skunks, armadillos, snake-eating snakes, and raptors commonly prey on this snake.

Venomous Texas Snakes

While the majority of snakes found in Texas are harmless, all should be treated with respect. It is important to distinguish between harmless snakes and venomous ones. The following snakes should be observed from a distance.

TEXAS CORAL SNAKE
Micrurus tener
The coral snake sports the familiar black, yellow, and red pattern that strikes fear into anyone's heart. While the pattern is mimicked by the harmless milk snakes, the coral snake's black on yellow band pattern is distinctive. Only about 50% of bites the coral snake inflicts actually contain venom, but all bites

"Black on yellow, kill a fellow" is an easy rhyme to remember the unique color pattern on the venomous coral snake.

that break the skin should be considered venomous and treated immediately by a qualified physician.

WESTERN COTTONMOUTH
Agkistrodon piscivorus leucostoma
Like rattlesnakes and copperheads, the Western cottonmouth has a triangular head, vertical pupils (like cat eyes), and a pit or depression on each side of the head. The cottonmouth is often associated with water, but can be found on dry land as well. A heavy-bodied snake, it can be identified in the water by its

The venomous western cottonmouth can be found both in the water or on land.

habit of lazily swimming in the water with its head slightly raised. In contrast, other (nonvenomous) snakes are quick and agile in the water. When threatened on land, the snake will often adopt an open-jawed threat posture. With the mouth open, you can easily see the distinctive creamy-white mouth that gives the cottonmouth its name. Another name for this species is water moccasin.

WESTERN DIAMONDBACK RATTLESNAKE AND OTHER RATTLESNAKES
Crotalus spp.

The wide, triangular head, vertical pupils, and pits (depressions on the head that look like a second, lower set of nostrils) of this western diamondback rattlesnake indicate that this snake is a venomous pit viper.

In addition to having a triangular head, vertical pupil, and pits, rattlesnakes also possess a rattle at the end of their tails. Rattlesnakes are often considered temperamental, and great care should be taken to avoid them.

THE COPPERHEADS
Agkistrodon spp.

Copperheads also have a triangular head, vertical pupils, and pits, but are distinctively colored and have light eyes.

Copperheads have the triangular head, vertical pupils, and pits of the other vipers, but are also colored with the distinctive brownish bands on a khaki background. Copperheads also have light eyes, which make the dark, vertical pupils easy to observe, even at a comfortable distance.

Amphibians

The chirping chorus of spring peepers or the booming throng of bullfrogs is a familiar sound from our childhood, recalling memories of spring campouts and sultry summer evenings. Amphibian species include toads, treefrogs, true frogs, spadefoot toads, burrowing toads, and salamanders. Frogs and toads are some of the easiest animals to attract to watery habitats since they need water for at least one part of their life cycle. Since frogs and salamanders breathe through their skin as well as with their lungs, provide these garden-friendly visitors with a fresh, clean source of water.

In addition, providing sturdy aquatic vegetation will give the frogs, toads, and salamanders a place to lay their eggs, and for the hatched young to grow to adulthood.

Amphibians like this spotted salamander are very beneficial to the garden, feeding on a variety of insects and spiders.

GULF COAST TOAD
Bufo valliceps

The Gulf Coast toad is found throughout east, central, and south Texas.

Marked by a broad dark stripe down each side and bordered above by a light stripe, this medium-sized flatish toad is found in most of East Texas and throughout Central and South Texas. Preferring a variety of moist habitats including backyard gardens, ditches, dump sites, and storm drains, it is most active at twilight, but can often be observed under street lights at night feasting on the insects attracted to the light. Breeding takes place from March to September.

The call of the delightful little green tree frog can be heard throughout east Texas on warm nights just before dark.

Spadefoot toads are so named for the short, hard spade located on the rear heel which is used for digging.

COPE'S GRAY TREEFROG AND GREEN TREEFROG
Hyla chrysoscelis, Hyla cinerea

These two species are almost identical in physical appearance, range, habitat, and behavior patterns, and can be differentiated only by close analysis of calls. These angular-looking treefrogs range in color from bright greenish yellow during the breeding season to dark gray when inactive or during cold weather. A showy white or pale yellow stripe runs along the side from the jaw to the groin, though sometimes this field mark is absent. Many have small golden flecks on their backs and their slim body is small and flat with prominent eyes and flashy white lips. They are found mainly in the eastern third of the state and prefer habitats with water, sandy banks, and dense vegetation. They call just before dark as they congregate in large choruses near the water. Preferring a variety of insects for food, they are frequently drawn toward lighted windows where insects are apt to be present.

COUCH'S SPADEFOOT TOAD
Scaphiopus couchii

Spadefoot toads take their name from the small, wedge-shaped "spades" found on their back legs. The Couch's Spadefoot can be found in grassland prairies and mesquite savannahs throughout the western two-thirds of Texas. Using the spades, it will dig deep and backward in the soil to rest under fallen logs, waiting for the drumbeat of rain hitting the soil above. When the rains come during the breeding season (April through September), the males dig themselves out, search for pools and puddles, then begin calling the silent females. Most mating happens the first night a pool forms, and young hatch, grow, and change into toadlets before the pool evaporates—leaving the pool only nine days after eggs are laid. The young will eat anything from algae to fairy shrimp, but adults dine on beetles, ants, grasshoppers, crickets, and other invertebrates.

Texas tortoise.

© William McCarley

© TPWD, Leroy Williamson

Often referred to as "creepy-crawlies," most insects and spiders are actually very beneficial to backyard habitats. Flying insects, such as honeybees and butterflies, drink the nectar from flowers as they pollinate. Wasps are often responsible for ridding the garden of a great deal of other pesky bugs such as ants, flies, spiders, and caterpillars. Beetles will often hunt for caterpillars, slugs, snails, and ants. Spiders prey on a variety of insects, using the familiar flying insect web trap of most spiders, or even actively hunting them down as the wolf spider does.

A green lacewing larva dines on whitefly nymphs.

© Courtesy USDA, Jack Dykinga

GREEN LACEWING
Family: *Chrysopidae*

The green lacewing adult is the "Tinker Bell" of the garden, with a clear green body and transparent wings laced with delicate green. While the adults, which grow to $^3/_4$ inch in length, are certainly the beauties, it is their less-than-pretty young that provide the most benefit to our gardens. The $^1/_2$-inch long, alligator-like larval forms of the lacewing delight in devouring all sorts of aphids, mealybugs, scale, and other small insects.

ANTLIONS
Family: *Myrmeleontidae*

The antlion larva waits in merciless ambush, but the adult form resembles a weak-flying damselfly.

© TPWD

All insects are interesting both in form and in behavior, but the antlion is a summer insect that can really pique your curiosity. The antlion most people recognize is not the adult, which resembles a weak-flying damselfly, but actually the larval form. The larvae spend their time at the bottom of a small, inverted cone-shaped pit built in fine-grained sand. You can often find the pits clustered together in sheltered areas near houses, rock ledges, and bridges. The pit is the "bug trap" that gives this diminutive insect its name. The edges of the pit are smooth, and ants, caterpillars, or other small crawling insects that venture too close to the pit fall in and have a great difficulty escaping. When the prey reaches the bottom of the pit, the antlion larva, which is buried just slightly under the surface, grasps it with its pinchers and injects it with a paralyzing venom, then sucks out the prey's juices. You can observe this action by using a piece of grass, pine needle, or other object to simulate a bug falling into the pit. You will observe the larva tossing dirt on top of the "capture," thus bringing it closer to the bottom. Once down at the bottom of the pit, the larva might even attempt to grasp the makeshift "prey."

The small inverted cones formed in fine-grained sand are often the only evidence of antlion larvae.

© TPWD, Jim Whitcomb

BLACK-AND-YELLOW ARGIOPE OR GARDEN SPIDER
Family Araneidae, subfamily *Argiopinae*

This large, colorful, and extremely visible creature is one of the more familiar spiders found in the garden. Known generically as the "garden spider," it is actually one of many brightly colored spiders that primarily inhabit grassy or weedy areas. The striped spiders construct large, vertical, orb-shaped webs which have a characteristic zigzag pattern running down the center. Called a "stabilimentum," this structure was once thought to provide stability to such a large web. While scientists aren't exactly sure what purpose the stabilimentum serves, various theories have arisen. Perhaps the wavy pattern camouflages a center-sitting

This striking garden spider, the black-and-yellow
Argiope, is a beautiful and beneficial addition to any
Wildscape.

The early-blooming Mexican plum tree (Prunus mexicana)
is a favorite with butterflies.

spider, or perhaps it makes the web more visible
to larger animals so they avoid moving through it.
Other theories question whether the structure could
allow the spider to adjust web tension or even serve
as "bait" to pollinating insects by imitating the reflective patterns of nectar-bearing flowers. Regardless of
the function of this intriguing structure, the Argiopes
are especially beneficial creatures, and should be trea-
sured in any Wildscape.

Butterflies

The image of butterfly wings flitting gingerly from
flower to flower like so many bits of confetti bobbing
in the sun can bring a smile to any gardener's face.
Butterflies add an ethereal beauty to flower gardens
and meadows and are second in importance only to
bees as plant pollinators. Together with the moths,
butterflies make up the second largest order of
insects, the Lepidoptera (from the Greek combining
forms "Lepido," meaning scale, and "ptera," meaning
wing). More than 17,500 species of butterflies have
been identified worldwide. While the greatest numbers are found in the tropical regions of the globe,

approximately 700 species of butterflies occur in
North America. Each region of the United States has
its characteristic butterfly fauna, and the butterflies
of a particular region often are specifically adapted
to the native plants of that region. Local field guides
and butterfly lists are increasingly available to those
wishing to know which species of butterflies are
common to an area and which native plant species
they use as nectar sources and larval host plants. (See
table 9.1 at the end of this chapter for a list of adult
and larval butterfly food sources in Texas.)

Butterflies and native plant species depend on one
another and help each other survive. While butterflies pollinate the flowers, the plants provide butterflies with food, housing, and sometimes chemical

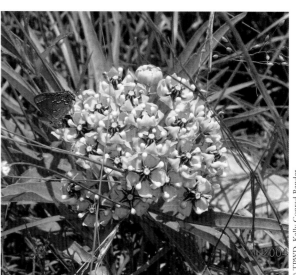

Some plants, such as this milkweed (Asclepias), can serve as both
larval host plants and adult nectar sources.

protection. The butterflies lay their eggs on appropriate host plants whose leaves provide ample food for the larvae. Nectar plants provide fuel for adults in their quest to find a mate and reproduce.

Planting local native plant species in a rich, well-planned butterfly garden will provide essential corridors between remaining patches of habitat and help repair the patchwork of healthy ecosystems that still exists. Every square meter devoted to a butterfly garden will also provide habitat for many other species of beneficial insects. Besides the conservation benefit, there is the added delight of watching butterflies flutter about the garden from the first warm days of spring to the last warm days of fall. As Robert Pyle, noted butterfly conservationist, expressed it, "The beauty of a swallowtail-studded patch of phlox confers a deep sense of pleasure that flowers alone are unable to match."

DESIGNING A BUTTERFLY GARDEN

Building a butterfly garden sanctuary around your home is not difficult. Whether you have a large house with extensive gardens and fields or a small garden apartment with a modest plot of yard space, anyone can attract and play host to butterflies. Much will depend on how enthusiastic you are and how strongly you can keep your need for neatness and order under control. Remember, though, that the design possibilities are limitless and need not conform to any particular model. You are completely free to create your own special vision, so experiment and have fun.

*Many different types of flowers can provide nectar to butterflies. This Queen butterfly is feeding from a buttonbush (*Cephalanthus occidentalis*).*

It is important to make the most of your natural setting. Butterflies like edges, for instance, so planting low flowers at the edge of a lawn, and high flowers at the edges of trees or along a fence is a way to enhance edge habitat. Locate a major part of the garden in a sunny, protected area. Butterflies are ectothermic (cold-blooded) and need sun to warm their body temperature. Place flat stones for butterflies to bask upon at various sunny locations in the garden. During cool mornings or cold spells, butterflies will perch on these stones or on bare soil to sun themselves. This behavior is necessary to raise their body temperature enough to allow them to fly. A few species of butterflies, such as the wood nymph and satyrs, prefer shady conditions, and if your yard has a wooded area, you might consider laying out special potions to attract these species. Geyata Ajilvsgi, in her publication *Butterfly Gardening for the South*, has a number of effective and apparently irresistible recipes.

Butterflies avoid high winds and appreciate windbreaks. If there are any natural structures to block the wind, leave them standing as butterflies will often congregate there on blustery days to get out of the wind. You may want to add tall plants to buffer the wind if your garden area does not possess natural barriers.

Native wildflowers serve as butterfly lures. Growing native species not only restores habitat, but also provides special nectar and larval food sources for the butterflies. When selecting wildflowers, it is always best to select those native to your region, though a few non-natives that do not become pesky weeds such as West Indian bloodroot *(Ascelpias curassavica)* and common butterfly-bush *(Buddleia* spp.*)*, or marigolds, do a magnificent job at attracting butterflies.

Most butterflies wander from place to place, stopping off temporarily at your garden to partake of food, water, and shelter on their way to somewhere else. When food sources disappear, butterflies go elsewhere. A combination of wildflowers and grasses that bloom from early spring through early fall will keep butterflies well fed throughout the seasons. Gardeners from the southeast and southwest Texas regions can enjoy amazingly extended flowering seasons with many attendant butterfly species, both residents and migrants.

You can provide butterflies with shelter by planting densely growing shrubbery, windbreaks, and by leaving snags and other cozy nooks in your Wildscape.

© TPWD, John Herron

In designing the layout of your garden, try to use large splashes of color. Butterflies are first attracted to flowers by their color, and a large mass of blooms is easier for them to spot. According to some experts, their favorite color is purple, followed by blue, yellow, white, pink, and orange. Members of the composite family of flowers, such as asters, coreopsis, boneset, goldenrods, and sunflowers are excellent nectar sources. How you group your colors, however, depends on your own preferences.

If you love butterflies, you will have to learn to love and provide for their larvae, too. Adult butterflies will definitely hang around if you feed and house their caterpillars. Admittedly, caterpillars look rather like worms—a life form not held in high regard by many people. It is important, however, to provide a good quantity of larval host plants for them, as larval food plants lure females into the garden to lay their eggs. Don't get overly attached to the larval host plants though, or you will be upset when you watch the hungry caterpillars eat them to shreds. That's how caterpillars grow. They will repay the plants indirectly by performing pollination duties at the next stage. It all evens out in the long run.

It is important to leave old trees as well as some younger trees, as butterflies like to perch on them and their larvae may use them for food. For instance, the beautiful swallowtail caterpillar prefers munching on the leaves of wild cherry. Mourning cloak caterpillars feed on elms and willows as well as hack-

berries. Spicebush caterpillars prefer, in addition to spicebush, red bay and sweet bay trees. Small trees, such as hawthorns, buckeyes, and sumacs offer nectar sources and shelter, as well. Try to leave thick brush under some of the trees, for this is where butterflies can find shelter and warmth on colder days or when it rains. These are also the areas where many species of caterpillars go to pupate.

A permanent wet patch or seep with various species of sedges and moisture-loving wildflowers will attract a multitude of butterflies. Provide damp areas or shallow puddles. If at all possible, install a seep irrigation system instead of sprinklers since sprinklers wash the nectar out of the flowers. A damp patch of sand, baited with a touch of manure or fermented fruit, will attract butterflies in a "puddle assemblage." Soil enriched by ashes from fires are especially attractive to them. Large congregations of "puddlers," mostly males who derive important elements from this foul feast, will descend to partake of the goodies. They will be less wary of observers here, and so it makes a good spot to take photos.

People who want to go all out might well choose to offer butterfly "delicacies"—which are anything but delicate. Beautiful butterflies do not always behave the way we might expect. Shunning our most prized roses, many prefer to feed on rotten fruit, carrion, mud puddles, oozing sap, human sweat, and even animal scat (fecal matter). Of course, this step is

© TPWD, Chuck Kowaleski

It is important to provide food for both larval (caterpillar) and adult butterflies in a Wildscape. Both the wooly bear caterpillar and the adult sulfur butterfly enjoy this salvia.

not for everyone, but if you choose to take it, you can attract species you might not otherwise see such as the dazzling red-spotted purple, hackberry, and goatweed butterflies. In fact, many attractive members of the Nymphalidae (brush-footed butterfly family) are attracted to these noisome buffets.

It is imperative that you not use insecticides anywhere near your butterfly garden, the larval food plants, or the adult nectar sources. These chemicals will kill butterflies in both the adult and larval stages. Treat any pest problem you have manually. If you have fire ants, try to use a juvenile growth hormone such as Logic, nontoxic insecticides like diatomaceous earth, or boiling water. Integrated pest management (see Chapter Four) is the best technique in any situation.

Remember, butterfly gardens develop gradually. They are not made overnight or even in one year. Each year you can increase the number of nectar plant selections and lengthen the blooming period to span the seasons. Planning, patience, and persistence are the keys to success. The more home gardeners add to the interactive communities of butterflies and native plants, the more stable and colorful the habitat will become.

SPICEBUSH SWALLOWTAIL
Papilio troilus

This beautiful, slow fluttering butterfly is a member of the Papilionidae family of butterflies. It is a black butterfly that measures about four inches from the tip of one wing to the other, and sports an iridescent patch of blue green on the hindwing. Pale yellow or green spots line the lower edges of the wings, and there is a small, spoon-shaped projection on the bottom edge of the hindwing. The range of the spicebush includes central and eastern Texas, and it prefers second-growth woods, deciduous woodlands, edges, wooded swamps, and pine barrens as habitat. You will often see the adult lazily fluttering about from April through October in search of its favorite nectar plants, including lantana, asters, cardinal flower, crownbeard, and salvias. The spicebush caterpillar prefers the vegetation of the spicebush, redbay, and sweetbay.

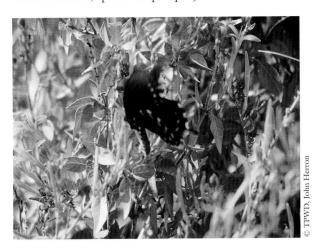

AMERICAN SNOUT
Libytheana carinenta

The unusual-looking American snout butterfly is a common inhabitant of Texas.

This little two-inch butterfly is easily recognizable by its "snout," which actually is its enlarged and beaklike labial palps (mouth parts). It flutters about at an incredible rate of speed, flashing a splash of orange on its upper wings. The underside of the wing, which you will see when the butterfly alights on a flower, is a mottled or solid gray. A typical behavior for the snout is to perch, head down, on a twig or small branch where it will mimic a dead leaf.

Look for the first brood of snouts flying in mid-May through June, and a second round of snouts in early August. The adults overwinter in South Texas and Florida, and the species sometimes will engage in spectacular migrations. The preferred larval food sources include desert hackberry and sugarberry species. The adult butterflies prefer dogwood, dogbane, and goldenrod for nectar.

With its large, easily identifiable wing patterns and spectacular migrations, the monarch butterfly is one of the most easily recognized butterflies in the United States.

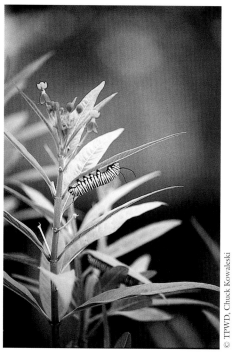

The monarch butterfly caterpillar is an unpalatable creature even to the hungriest birds.

MONARCH
Danaus plexippus

The monarch butterfly is perhaps the most commonly recognized butterfly in North America. Ranging in size from $3\frac{1}{2}$ to $4\frac{1}{2}$ inches, the monarch's wings are a beautiful bright orange with black veins and a black border with two rows of white dots. The monarch is found throughout Texas and undergoes dramatic migrations. Millions of adult butterflies spend their winter in colonies in central Mexico. The larval monarch butterflies are dependent on milkweed plant species for food, and the adults store a poison from the milkweed which, in turn, makes them extremely unpalatable to birds. The adult butterflies feed on a variety of flowers, including lantana, boneset, frostweed, sunflowers, and groundsel. The habitat of the Monarch includes open, weedy areas, roadsides, pastures, marshes, and other similar areas.

With its thread of "gold," even the monarch chrysalis is beautiful.

Table 9.1

* Not native to Texas, but not invasive.

Species	Larval Food Plants	Adult Food Plants (Nectar Sources)
Black Swallowtail	Prairie parsley, Dutchman's breeches, bishop's weed, dill*, parsley*, fennel*, carrot*	Fruit tree blossoms, lantana, boneset, asters, thistles, milkweeds, clover
Bordered Patch	Sunflower, crownbeard, ragweeds, straggler daisy, cockleburs	Sunflowers, crownbeard, ragweeds, straggler daisy, cockleburs, composites
Common Buckeye	Purple gerardia, paintbrush, frog-fruit, ruellia, snapdragon, plantain, toadflax	Purple gerardia, paintbrush, frog-fruit, ruellia, lantana, composites
Cloudless Sulphur	Senna species, partridge pea, cassia	Lantana, hibiscus, turk's cap, cardinal flower tropical sage, goldenrod
Common Checkered-Skipper	Globe mallow, common mallow, sida, hollyhocks, hibiscus	Milkweeds, dandelions, asters, frog-fruit, and fleabane
Southern Dogface	Leadplant, clover species, alfalfa, prairie clover	Verbena, golden-wave, bur-clover, salvias
Falcate Orangetip	Rockcress, peppergrass, rocket mustard	Violet species, chickweed, and Prunus species
Giant Swallowtail	Lime prickly-ash, hop-tree, cultivated citrus, trifoliate orange, Hercules'-club	Lantana, butterfly-bush, milkweeds, honeysuckles. Also partakes of fruit juices and manure.
Great Southern White	Peppergrass, members of the mustard family, shepherd's purse	Eclectic tastes
Great Purple Hairstreak	Mostly mistletoe, eastern cottonwood, mesquite, sycamore	Roosevelt weed, creek plum, Mexican plum, goldenrods, ragweeds
Gulf Fritillary	Passion-flower species, passion-vine	Butterfly bush, lantana, boneset, golden-eye, asters
Goatweed Leafwing	Silver croton, one-seed croton, woolly croton	Likes tree sap, juices of fruits, moisture from decaying wood
Hackberry Emperor	Hackberry species	Prefers carrion, dung, tree sap, rotting fruit, and mud
Crimson Patch	Flame acanthus	Flame acanthus, bee-brush, annual sunflower
Julia Helicanian	Passion-flower, passion vine	Lantana species
Common Wood Nymph	Wild petunia, waterwillow and various grasses	Boneset, milkweeds, thistles, golden-eye, clematis, button-bush
Long-tailed Skipper	Legumes and mustards	Legumes and mustards
Monarch	Milkweed species, milkweed vine	Lantana, boneset, frostweed, sunflowers, groundsels, Roosevelt weed, goldeneye
Mourning Cloak	Black willow, eastern cottonwood, hackberries	Milkweeds and goldenrods

Table 9.1, cont.

COMMON TEXAS BUTTER,Y SPECIES AND NECTAR PLANT SOURCES

* Not native to Texas, but not invasive.

Species	Larval Food Plants	Adult Food Plants (Nectar Sources)
Painted Lady	Thistles, milfoil, globemallow, and mugwort	Thistles, milfoil, mugwort, gayfeathers, asters
Palamedes Swallowtail	Red bay, sweet bay, and sassafras	Thistles, phlox, verbenas, azaleas*, pickerel-weed, yellow iris, purple loosestrife
Pipevine Swallowtail	Dutchman's pipe	Lantana, phlox, frostweed, cardinal flower, thistles, butterfly bush, sand-verbena, and frost-weed
Queen	Milkweed species	Milkweed species, frog fruit, blue mistflower, boneset
Question Mark	Nettles, hackberries, cedar elm	Likes mud, tree sap, carrion, also asters and milkweeds
Red Admiral	Nettles, false nettle, pellitory	Milkweeds, asters, dogbanes, bonesets, tree sap, ripe fruit, animal dung
Red-spotted Purple	Black cherry, eastern cottonwood, basswood, ironwood, hop-hornbeam	Eclectic tastes, likes carrion, dung, floral nectar, rotten fruit, tree sap, insect honeydew
American Snout	Hackberry species	Dogwood, dogbane species, goldenrods
Spicebush Swallowtail	Spicebush, red bay, sweet bay, sassafras, and tulip tree	Lantana, asters, cardinal flower, phlox, verbenas, crownbeard, salvias, bee balm, and bergamot
Texas Crescent	Flame acanthus, orega de raton, dicliptera, ruellia	Kidneywood, boneset, golden-eye, Indian blanket
Eastern Tiger Swallowtail	Green ash, Mexican plum, blackcherry, eastern cottonwood, camphor-tree	Butterfly weed, butterfly bush, abelia*, azaleas*, salvias, milkweeds
Variegated Fritillary	Stiff-stem flax, violets, pansies, purselane, and passion flowers	Flax species
Zebra Heliconian	Passion-flowers, passion flower vines	Mistflower, lantana, bonesets, golden-eye, varied tastes
Zebra Swallowtail	Common pawpaw, dwarf pawpaw, big flowered pawpaw	Pawpaw, turk's cap

Part 3
GARDEN TROUBLESHOOTING

© TPWD, Chuck Kowaleski

© TPWD, Bill Reaves

While the benefits of establishing a backyard habitat to attract wildlife are substantial, there are a few drawbacks. As our towns grow and suburbs expand, there will be inevitable conflicts between the needs of people and the needs of animals. And, while wildlife is a source of enjoyment for most urban residents, some wildlife species can be a source of frustration, annoyance, and even fear for people.

The sight of white-tailed deer browsing nonchalantly on your prized flowering shrubs or cottontails munching in your garden is unsettling to say the least. Beavers clogging up streams or drainage ways, raccoons invading your attic to raise their families, opossums camping out in your garbage can, armadillos rooting for insects, and snakes under the house are outright nuisances. These types of problems may arise whether you landscape for wildlife or not, but a well-designed Wildscape can help you attract desirable species and deter nuisance behavior of others.

Of course, no plan can eliminate all problems. Tolerance for small levels of inconvenience and frustration may be the price we need to pay for the benefits we receive in bringing wildlife into our lives. Fortunately, the Texas Department of Agriculture has an effective program called Texas Wildlife Services with a staff of biologists trained in methods to control or deter nuisance animals. Wildlife Services staff can also offer technical assistance in trapping unwanted wildlife. Your local office can be located by calling the state office in San Antonio at 210-472-5451.

RACCOONS

The wily raccoon, at once an endearing charmer and mischievous masked bandito, can be a delightful source of entertainment, but also an extreme annoyance. The autumn begins with a restless search for a winter den, and in the summer the female seeks out a safe haven to rear her young. If your house or apartment is not well sealed or if your garbage cans are not battened down well, you can count on faithful families of raccoons sharing your living space. These masked critters are driven by an insatiable curiosity and a voracious appetite to rummage through your garbage or your pet's outside food bowl for leftovers. They will pick through the bounty, examining the best pieces with their forepaws, then wash them in the dog's water bowl before eating.

The nightly raids can be entertaining to watch when it takes place on your porch, but their persistent thumping and scratching about in your attic or kitchen is disturbing. If you want to deter raccoons, equip your garbage cans with screen door spring guards, don't leave cat or dog food and water outside at night, and make sure your home is securely sealed. A convenient pet entrance for your dog or cat is like an open invitation to these clever explorers who will quickly gain access to and rummage through your cabinets. Control methods include trapping and repellents, but prevention is more than half the cure. Screen attic and foundation access points to prevent them from getting in or under the house. Feed your pets during the day and remove leftovers before nightfall. Take bird feeders down and empty water bowls at night.

ARMADILLOS

These armored creatures are really quite interesting—until you wake up one morning and see the damage they've done to your gardens and yard. From the armadillo's point of view, rooting around looking for succulent roots, bulbs, and tasty insects is the normal thing to do. But what a mess it leaves! Some homeowners tolerate the digging, while others resent the intrusion. About the size of an

© TPWD

The comical raccoon is an increasingly common wild animal in urban and suburban areas.

© TPWD, Leroy Williamson

The prehistoric-looking armadillo digs in the soil looking for grubs, tubers, and roots.

opossum, armadillos normally produce one litter a year. They are active primarily from twilight through early morning hours in the summer and during the day only during the winter. Their favorite diet consists of larval beetles, termites, ants, and other invertebrates. They may also eat fruit and vegetable matter. Because of their diet they are actually beneficial animals, but unfortunately lawns, gardens, and flower beds are often their preferred hunting grounds.

When armadillo damage is significant, there are a few things you can do to keep your garden intact. First, look at your soil. If you have a good balance of predatory and beneficial organisms, there will be less armadillo prey. Complete exclusion of armadillos can only be achieved by installing a strong fence and burying the bottom at least 1 foot in the ground. A less expensive method is to put foul smelling rags or cotton balls (vinegar and ammonia work well) where armadillos are digging. Do not use mothballs, as they release toxic chemicals that will damage the ecosystem and potentially your own health. It is reported that armadillos also tend to avoid areas with pine needles or pine mulch. Live-trapping and moving should be considered a last resort, but if you use this method traps should be about large housecat size, and can be baited with mealy worms in a nylon stocking sack.

BEAVERS

Beavers can cause property damage by gnawing on and killing ornamental trees.

Because beavers are actually rodents, they must continually gnaw to wear down their front teeth.

The beaver is the largest rodent in North America and an industrious dam builder, admirable for his work ethic and engineering skills. Beavers commonly reside in lakes, rivers, streams, and other aquatic environments that contain an adequate flow of water for damming. Beavers must continually gnaw trees to keep their front teeth from growing into their skulls.

The major concern of homeowners and farmers is that as the land behind a beaver dam is flooded, shorelines can also be damaged. The animals also build caches (hiding places for food piles) with the branches of deciduous trees and will sometimes injure or kill ornamental or fruit trees. On many streams and ponds, you can encourage beavers to go elsewhere by removing food trees and dam construction material from the water's edge. Try excluding beavers from a plot of land by erecting a metal fence around property and by fencing of culverts, drain pipes, or other structures. Shield ornamental trees by wrapping each one in wire mesh, hardware cloth, or tree wrap. You can also mix a recipe of one tablespoon of hot pepper sauce in a gallon of water and spray it on tree trunks to reduce gnawing damage to the trees. When beavers are active during warm months, you need to reapply the compound periodically. If trapping is used, special traps must be used due to the beaver's size, strength, and sharp incisors. Traps are expensive and take skill to set properly, and it is often it is hard to catch all members of the family.

NUTRIA

Introduced from South America as "aquatic weed cutters," nutria are large, semiaquatic rodents that

The nutria is an introduced species originally from South America.

consume a wide range of animal and plant foods. They will also scavenge any carrion and garbage available. Opossums are furbearers and are classified as a game species in some states, but not in Texas. While they sometimes cause damage similar to skunks and raccoons, overall the level of damage they cause is slight, and they are beneficial as scavengers. The best control measure for opossums is exclusion. Many of the same methods used for raccoons will work for opossums: secure trash containers with tight-fitting lids and pick up leftover pet food at night if you feed your pets outside.

resemble beavers and muskrats. Almost exclusively vegetarian, they consume about three pounds of food a day. Nutria damage occurs when they eat desirable vegetation and girdle ornamental trees. They can also dig their burrows into pond dams, levees, or watershed structures which may weaken the structures and cause them to collapse. Habitat manipulation and good farming practices such as aquatic weed control and proper drainage maintenance are good strategies for discouraging nutria from getting established in the first place. Nutria are classified as furbearers in Texas, but it is legal to trap them if they are causing damage. There are several trap styles available. Snares are sometimes used when other trapping methods are not feasible.

OPOSSUMS

Our only marsupial, opossums are especially appealing when they are young. While they sport a mouth full of teeth, they are really shy and inoffensive animals. However, they can be a nuisance when they raid the garbage. Opossums are omnivores and will

RABBITS

There is no doubt about it, bunnies are cute, but they can also be quite destructive in the backyard vegetable garden. Eastern cottontails and their relatives are generally found in brushy hedgerows and wood edges with dense cover. They also do well in urban areas and suburbs with shrubs, gardens, and lawns. Renown for their reproductive capabilities, rabbits feed on leafy plants during the growing season and the buds and bark of woody plants during the winter. Sometimes in the spring they do damage to vegetable and flower gardens. A well-constructed fence around your garden is the most effective permanent protection against rabbit damage. It need only be two feet high and made of one-inch poultry wire stretched from post to post. The lower edges should be staked securely to the ground or slightly buried. Protect small garden plots and individual plants by applying chemical repellents that rabbits find distasteful, or consider modifying the habitat. Rabbits avoid areas with little cover because of the danger from predators. Live trapping of rabbits and relocating them is

The Virginia opossum is North America's only marsupial.

The Eastern cottontail finds a home in brushy hedgerows, woody edges with dense cover, and urban and suburban areas with shrubs, gardens, and lush lawns.

a temporary solution, since replacements will soon arrive. Locate trapped rabbits to suitable locations immediately to avoid self-inflicted injuries.

BATS

There are thirty-two species of bats recorded in Texas, each with distinctive physical characteristics and life-style. Those few species that roost in or on buildings, whether in colonies or singly, are the only bats people are likely to encounter. These species are attracted to suburban and urban areas where there are substantial populations of flying insects. Most bats feed on insects which they catch in flight. Bats are particularly important in the control of night-flying insects. A single bat can consume 2,000 or more insects in one night. Large colonies of bats are thus extremely important for insect control. Like any mammal, bats are susceptible to rabies. However, less than one-half of one percent of bats in North America ever contract the disease.

If you have bats in your attic, the only permanent way to remove them is by excluding their entrances after they have vacated the premises. Chemicals should never be used. They are expensive, temporary, and cause worse problems by exposing the neighborhood to sick and dying bats. Any removal of bats should be done by the methods described in Merlin Tuttle's book, *America's Neighborhood Bats*. These techniques are very effective and inexpensive. For more information about bats, refer to the Bat Conservation International Web Site (www.batcon.org).

The Mexican free-tailed bats, which are common in central Texas, can consume 2,000 insects per bat per night.

STARLINGS AND GRACKLES

Grackles thrive in the vast expanses of lawn in suburban and urban areas.

Often forming huge roosts in urban areas, starlings and grackles flock together during the fall, winter, and early spring. While individual birds normally do not pose much of a problem, they can be a real nuisance when they flock together and roost in trees near homes and public facilities. While grackles can consume or destroy some farm crops, the smaller European starlings are far more aggressive. They were introduced into New York from Europe in the late 1800s. This was an unfortunate idea and a harmful introduction, as this opportunistic bird has outcompeted many of our native species such as woodpeckers and bluebirds for nesting spots. They can also cause damage to orchards and gardens. There are several methods available for discouraging roosting birds. Thinning roost vegetation and decreasing lawn area, thereby making it less attractive to the birds, often produces longer lasting results than scare tactics. For additional information and technical assistance with the control of roosting birds, contact your local Texas Wildlife Services specialist.

SNAKES

Texas has many different kinds of snakes—only the Western cottonmouth, the Texas coral snake, copperheads, and rattlesnakes are venomous to humans. Of those snakes that share human habitats, most are harmless. Snakes perform many valuable ecological services and are often maligned due to fear and

Snakes are an important component of ecological systems.

misinformation. Many harmless snakes are killed for no better reason than it seems the thing to do.

Like other reptiles, snakes are ectothermic (cold-blooded). They cannot tolerate extremely cold temperatures, and they will normally hibernate during the winter months. Since most are active at night and during early morning and late evening hours, they usually escape notice. If you absolutely cannot tolerate the presence of snakes, there are various control methods available. One of the most effective methods is to remove their shelter. Eliminating rock piles, brush piles and tall grass will cause them to seek a more suitable habitat elsewhere. Store wood piles and lumber at least eighteen inches off the ground. You can eliminate their food supply by controlling insect and rodent populations around the house. Exclusion is another important strategy in deterring snakes. Keep snakes out of houses and other buildings by sealing all points of entry. Trapping is also an effective method of catching snakes that have taken up residence inside the house. Captured snakes can then be released elsewhere.

DEER

The sight of a white-tailed deer feeding in the front yard is a delight to many. However, in some suburban areas of Texas where human habitation has benefited deer, the population of these animals has gotten out of control. Many times, deer will exceed the carrying capacity, or the maximum population numbers that a given area can support. When this happens, they are forced into yards and gardens to get the food they need to survive. Well-tended, well-watered gardens are a delicious bonanza for these animals, especially during the drought periods of summer when the browse (thin branches) in

An overpopulation of white-tailed deer can devastate suburban gardens.

the wild has been seriously diminished. Exclusion by deer-proof fencing is probably the best method of keeping hungry deer from eating your plants and trees. If you feed deer, it only makes the situation worse by producing more deer than the habitat can support since food is quickly translated into new fawns which creates even larger deer populations. Without natural population controls, such as mountain lions, wolves, and screw-worm disease, the land can soon be overrun with a glut of deer. (See the list of "deer-resistant" native plants in chapter eleven.)

CATS

Cats today rank as American's favorite pet, and there are over three million domestic cats in Texas. Many of these cats are free-ranging pet cats, stray cats, and feral cats (domestic cats living in the wild). As beautiful and playful as they might be, domestic cats are efficient predators of birds, small mammals, reptiles, and amphibians when left to their own devices. While loss of habitat and pollution of the air and water are cited as major causes of declines of bird species, domestic and feral cats are also a factor, especially in urban and suburban areas. No matter how well a cat is fed, it will still kill birds. That is the

Domestic cats are efficient hunters of native wildlife. Keeping a cat indoors will help prevent excessive predation.

nature of cats. Indeed, after sleeping, hunting is the favorite pastime of cats. However, cats are not "natural" predators since they occur in higher numbers than would be possible for a wild predator. Many cats are fed by humans, and so are not totally dependent on prey numbers to support their growing population.

Cats first accompanied the British colonists as early as 1614 when they arrived on American shores and were imported again in the 1800s to assist in rodent control. The introduction of foreign species into a new territory frequently has negative effects on native species' populations. Domestic cats are no exception. Feral cats have caused their share of damage, especially on small islands where they have brought about the extinction of native birds. Ground-nesting birds like the wood thrush and chuck-will's-widow are especially vulnerable, and young fledglings are literally "sitting ducks" to a cat. Feral, stray, and free-ranging pet cats roaming Texas is a very real problem. Unwanted kittens cast off into the woods must fend for themselves and live off the land. Their expanding population puts tremendous pressure on native wildlife. Cat prey items include rodents, birds, rabbits, reptiles and amphibians, and insects. In fact, a rural cat will kill an average of eighty-three animals per year, and an urban cat will kill an average of twenty-six animals a year. This is tremendous predation, especially considering that cats outnumber all other mammalian predators combined. It is unfair to attract birds to your backyard if cats are allowed to stalk them at will.

CURBING THE CAT PROBLEM

If you have a cat, there are several things you can do to help save birds and other wildlife while also watching out for the best interest of your cat.

🐾 Make your kitty an indoor cat. Remember, bells are ineffective wildlife warning devices, and by keeping your cat inside, you are protecting him from disease, parasites, fleas, ticks, and serious injury. Cats gradually introduced back into homelife will not only be much healthier than their outdoor compatriots, but will also be quite happy and content.

🐾 Only about 20% of America's cats have been spayed or neutered, yet cats are prolific breeders. Have your cat neutered or spayed in a timely manner.

🐾 Support programs to remove cats that are living off the land in parks and refuges.

🐾 Never dump unwanted kittens into the nearby woods. Take them to the humane society or have a kitty sale. Dumping kittens into the wild is cruel both to the kittens and to the birds, reptiles, and small mammals that will serve as their food.

🐾 Don't abandon a pet cat when moving to new premises. Take the time to find it a new home.

DISCOURAGING NEST BOX PREDATORS

Nest boxes and feeders undeniably offer much-needed feeding and nesting resources in our backyards, but by providing these predictable, easily recognized structures for animals to feed at and nest in, we also provide easily patrolled hunting areas for predators such as snakes, raccoons, opossums, and house cats. Moreover, these coveted areas are often scouted out by aggressive species such as house sparrows, European starlings, and grackles, who then oust desirable species from the nesting cavities or chase them from their feeding areas.

Prevent snakes, raccoons, and other predators from accessing nest boxes by installing a baffle around the nest box pole (figure 10a). Construct the baffle out of 26-gauge sheet metal in either a cone or cylinder shape. Place the baffle on the nest box pole, as high off the ground or water surface as possible and about six to twelve inches below the nest box for a cylinder-type baffle, and at least three feet from the ground or water surface for a cone-type baffle. To prevent predation by snakes and mammals, place a 6" length of appropriate diameter PVC pipe into the entrance hole of the nest box (figure 10b).

The house sparrow is a cheerful exotic bird that has adapted well to urban life. Unfortunately, it is also very aggressive, and takes over the nesting sites of many native birds.

FIGURE 10A

FIGURE 10B

HOUSE SPARROWS AND EUROPEAN STARLINGS

House sparrows and European starlings are both aggressive and exotic (not native to Texas or the United States) species that aggressively run off other native species from both natural and artificially provided nesting areas. These avian tyrants sometimes even kill the native species to retain the coveted nesting spot. Neither the house sparrow nor the European starling is protected in the United States, and should be evicted from nest boxes. Often, you will have to remove the same pair several times before they get the message and leave your area for good.

Entrances to nest boxes are accessible to house sparrows if they are at least $1\frac{3}{8}$" in diameter, and to European starlings if they are at least $1\frac{1}{2}$" in diameter, so be sure to construct nest box entrances at the smallest size possible. Also, do not provide perches for bird nest boxes, since the sparrows and starlings seem to prefer houses with this feature.

The European starling is an introduced bird which competes directly with native birds for suitable nest sites.

Prevent wasps from attaching their nest to the roof of nest boxes by rubbing layers of liquid soap or rubbing a bar of soap on the inside ceiling.

WASP NESTS

If wasps or other insects invade the nest box before it can be occupied by birds, try to remove the nest manually (armed with a can of insecticide for self-protection), or spray the box with pyrethrin which is not toxic to birds, and plug the hole for twenty-four hours. To prevent wasps from attaching a nest to the roof of the nest box, rub regular bar soap on the box ceilings.

FIRE ANTS

The red imported fire ant *(Solenopsis invicta)* is an introduced species which is extremely detrimental to many species of native wildlife, including nesting birds. You can protect your nesting birds from fire ants in three ways. One effective method is to "grease" the support pole with a mixture of five pounds chassis grease and one quart of turpentine (mixed well). If the support pole is wooden, apply a layer of duct tape first to prevent the wood from absorbing the mixture. Be sure to check the application periodically to ensure that it is still tacky and effective. Another way to prevent ants from crawling up to the nest box is to apply a layer of DE (Diatomaceous Earth), which is a nontoxic product that kills many different insects by cutting the insects' waxy exoskeleton and absorbing the insects' body liquid. DE kills a wide variety of insects, including beneficial insects, so its use should be restricted to areas of infestation or where potential infestation would cause great harm (such as around a nest box). The third method of fire ant control is to use Logic® insect growth regulator. Since Logic® is specific to ants, it does not harm "nontarget" organisms. Logic® can be used either as a single mound treatment or as a broadcast application, and is typically targeted at the red imported fire ant and big-headed ant *(Pheidole megacephaia)* colonies.

The red imported fire ant is not only a bother at picnics, it is also deadly to many species of native wildlife.

© Chuck Kowaleski

© TPWD,Glenn Mills

In Texas, there is no such thing as a "typical yard." Our landscapes have shaded areas, soggy spots, and sections that are overrun with hungry deer. What do you do with these problem areas when planting a Wildscape? Turn your trouble spots into assets by accentuating them, flaunting them, and making them the highlight of your garden!

Those shaded areas, when properly planned, can be transformed into the jewels of your yard. Turn that dappled shade garden into a hideaway that replicates a deep forest draped in bracken fern *(Pteridium aquilinum)*, carpeted with delicate partridgeberry *(Mitchella repens)*, and punctuated with vibrant widow's tears *(Tinantia anomala)*. Turn soggy areas into shallow bogs or wetlands just big enough to entice butterflies to "puddle" or gather by the moist edges. Your wetland might also attract a few wading birds anxious to gobble up the invertebrates, such as dragonfly larvae, in the mud. For that matter, why try to do battle with the deer? By planting vegetation that deer avoid, you will enjoy a hardy, beautiful, and mostly "unmunched" garden.

Shady Areas

Selecting plant species for shaded areas can present a real challenge for home gardeners. You may have a few areas that are so shady that even the most shade-tolerant species won't thrive. While some Texas natives do well under a variety of lighting conditions, the majority of plants have distinct lighting preferences.

FULL SUN: Full sun means that the plants grow best when exposed to direct sunlight all day long. Many native Texas wildflowers prefer full sun, yet some of these sun lovers can tolerate shade for a couple of hours (but no more than that).

This lovely shrubby boneset will thrive in areas with dappled shade.

PARTIAL SHADE: Plants in this category prefer the morning sun, which is less intense, from four to six hours per day.

DAPPLED SHADE: Dappled shade occurs when sunlight is filtered through the leaves of trees and is patchy most of the time. Many shade-loving plants thrive and bloom in a half-day or more of dappled shade.

SHADE: Shade-loving species can tolerate as little as two hours of direct sun or four hours of dappled sunshine per day. Many of these species also require additional moisture if placed in sunnier spots. Various native forbs (nonwoody, nongrassy plants, such as wildflowers), grasses, vines, and shrubs will thrive in shady or semishady situations.

The American beautyberry is a wonderful understory plant. In the spring the loosely-shaped shrub produces delicate pink flowers. In the fall, the flowers yield vibrant purple berries.

SELECTING SHADE TOLERANT PLANTS
Before purchasing and planting new vegetation, analyze how much shade your yard gets in various locations during different seasons, then learn which plants will grow and thrive under these conditions (see table 11.1 at the end of this chapter).

Wet Area Gardening

It is obvious that Texas is blessed with scenic vistas, rolling prairies, and towering forests. However, the quantity and variety of aquatic habitats found within Texas' borders are also impressive. Swiftly moving streams, quiet bogs, and gently flowing rivers are only part of the rich diversity of Texas' aquatic habitats. Re-create natural aquatic habitat in your yard by turning soggy areas and water sources into wetlands and oases. Select native Texas plants, and make your yard abuzz with wildlife activity.

AQUATIC PLANTS

Lady fern
  Athyrium filix-femina
Buttonbush
  Cephalanthus occidentalis
Crinum lily
  Crinum americanum
Titi
  Cyrilla racemiflora
White-topped sedge
  Rhynchospora colorata
Horsetail
  Equisetum hyemale
Swamp sunflower
  Helianthus angustifolius
Waterleaf
  Hydrolea ovata
Chain fern
  Woodwardia areolata
Yellow lotus
  Nelumbo lutea

White water-lily
  Nymphaea odorata
Floating-heart
  Nymphoides aquatica
Sensitive fern
  Onoclea sensibilis
Cinnamon fern
  Osmunda cinnamomea
Royal fern
  Osmunda regalis var. *spectabilis*
Tuckahoe
  Peltandra virginica
Pickerel-weed
  Pontederia cordata
Arrowhead
  Sagittaria lancifolia
Lizard's-tail
  Saururus cernuus
Powdery thalia
  Thalia dealbata
Meadow-rue
  Thalictrum sp.
Narrowleaf cattail
  Typha angustifolia
Floating bladderwort
  Utricularia radiata
Virginia chain fern
  Woodwardia virginica

© TPWD, John Herron

Ponds edged and filled with plants will provide habitat for a variety of birds, amphibians, dragonflies, and more!

Dealing with Deer

The white-tailed deer *(Odocoileus virginianus)* is by far the most abundant large native herbivore in Central Texas. In fact, deer are more numerous today than they were when North America was first settled by Europeans. Several factors have contributed to the burgeoning deer population in our region, including the eradication of screwworm disease, the reduction of natural predators such as wolves and mountain lions, and the widespread practice by well-meaning homeowners of setting out supplemental food for them.

As creatures of the forest edge, deer are highly adaptable to the environmental changes wrought by man. White tails prefer a diverse habitat with a mixture of forage and cover. If there is an adequate supply of natural browse (tender shoots, twigs, and leaves) in the deer's usual feeding ground, they will likely not touch a homeowner's ornamental or vegetable garden. If, on the other hand, the natural food supply is low due to extended drought or other adverse environmental conditions, deer will boldly invade our well-tended domestic gardens.

The white-tailed deer has adapted very well to the environmental changes brought on by humans.

HIGHLY PALATABLE PLANTS

Deer, like most animals, are selective in their foraging, avoiding some species while seeking out others with relish. They eat a wide variety of vegetation and change their diet according to what is available. A hungry deer will avoid a particular plant depending primarily on the availability of other food; but you can better your odds of growing a green Wildscape by eliminating those plants that deer find absolutely irresistible.

PALATABLE PLANTS TO AVOID

Roses
Pansies
Pyracantha spp.
Spirea spp.
Hibiscus
Petunias
Euonymous
Photinia spp.
Geraniums

SELECTING DEER-RESISTANT PLANTS

Only a few plants are so toxic or distasteful that deer will avoid them altogether. Others are avoided only at certain stages of growth, with palatability varying with the plant's age or with the seasons. Under stress, however, few plants are totally resistant to the white-tailed deer. And where deer pressure is very high, even unpalatable plants will be devoured. Selecting wildflowers in an effort to "deer-proof" your planting may improve their survival, but nothing will guarantee their safety after a hard winter or spring in an area of intense population pressure (see table 11.2 at the end of this chapter).

Mexican hat.

Table 11.1
PLANTS THAT ACCEPT VARIABLE DEGREES OF SHADE

Common name	Scientific name	Shade	Dappled	Partial	Full sun
Flowers					
Wild Red Columbine	*Aquilegia canadensis*	X	X	X	
Annual Aster	*Symphyotrichum subulatum*				X
Texas Aster	*Symphyorichum drummondii*		X	X	X
Winecup	*Callirhoe involucrata*			X	X
Straggler Daisy	*Calyptocarpus vialis*	X	X	X	X
Wild Hyacinth	*Camassia scilloides*		X	X	
Day-flower	*Commelina erecta*		X	X	
False Day-flower	*Tinantia anomala*		X	X	
Rainlilies	*Cooperia* spp.	X	X	X	
Spectacle-pod	*Dimorphocarpa wislizenii*		X	X	
Wild Buckwheat	*Eriogonum multiflorum*		X	X	
Blue Mistflower	*Conoclinium coelestinum*		X	X	
White Avens	*Geum canadense*	X	X	X	
Standing Cypress	*Ipomopsis rubra*		X	X	X
Copper Lily	*Habranthus tubispathus*		X	X	
Cardinal Flower	*Lobelia cardinalis*		X	X	
Coral Honeysuckle	*Lonicera sempervirens*			X	
Partridgeberry	*Mitchella repens*	X	X	X	
Baby Blue-eyes	*Nemophila phacelioides*		X	X	
Yellow Passionflower	*Passiflora lutea*		X	X	
Rose Pavonia	*Pavonia lasiopetala*			X	X
Gulf Coast Foxglove	*Penstemon tenuis*		X	X	X
Blue Curls	*Phacelia congesta*		X	X	X
Drummond's Phlox	*Phlox drummondii*		X	X	X
Fragrant Phlox	*Phlox pilosa*		X	X	
Texas Frog-fruit	*Phyla nodiflora*		X	X	X
Obedient Plant	*Physostegia angustifolia*		X	X	
White Milkwort	*Polygala alba*		X	X	X
Pidgeonberry	*Rivina humilis*	X	X	X	
Common Ruellia, Wild Petunia	*Ruellia nudiflora*		X	X	
Meadow-pink	*Sabatia campestris*		X	X	X
Scarlet Sage	*Salvia coccinea*		X	X	X
Autumn Sage	*Salvia greggii*			X	
Lyreleaf Sage	*Salvia lyrata*		X	X	
Golden Groundsel	*Packera obovata*	X	X	X	
Blue-eyed Grass	*Sisyrinchium* spp.		X	X	
American Germander	*Teucrium canadense*	X	X	X	
Spiderworts	*Tradescantia* spp.	X	X	X	

Common name	Scientific name	Shade	Dappled	Partial	Full sun
Western Ironweed	*Vernonia baldwinii*		X	X	X
Hairy Zexmania	*Wedelia texana*		X	X	X
Grasses and grasslike plants					
Cedar-sedge	*Carex planostachys*	X	X		
Inland Seaoats	*Chasmanthium latifolium*	X	X	X	
Canada Wildrye	*Elymus canadensis*		X	X	
Vines					
Crossvine	*Bignonia capreolata*	X	X	X	X
Trumpet-vine	*Campsis radicans*			X	X
Scarlet Clematis	*Clematis texensis*	X	X	X	
Snapdragon Vine	*Maurandella antirrhiniflora*		X	X	
Virginia Creeper	*Parthenocissus quinquefolia*	X	X	X	
Shrubs					
American Beautyberry	*Callicarpa americana*	X	X	X	
Chili Pequín	*Capsicum annuum*	X	X	X	
New Jersey Tea	*Ceanothus americanus*		X	X	
Deciduous Holly	*Ilex decidua*		X	X	
Yaupon	*Ilex vomitoria*		X	X	X
Wax-myrtle	*Morella cerifera*	X	X	X	
Texas Mock Orange	*Philadelphus texensis*		X	X	X
Fragrant Sumac	*Rhus aromatica*		X	X	X
Pidgeonberry	*Rivina humilis*		X	X	
Eve's Necklace	*Sophora affinis*		X	X	X
Carolina Cherry Laurel	*Prunus caroliniana*		X	X	
Texas Mountain Laurel	*Sophora secundiflora*	X	X	X	
Mexican Buckeye	*Ungnadia speciosa*		X	X	X
Texas Persimmon	*Diospyros texana*	X	X	X	X
Rusty Blackhaw Viburnum	*Viburnum rufidulum*			X	X
Woods Rose	*Rosa woodsii*		X	X	X
Coralberry	*Symphoricarpos orbiculatus*		X	X	
Virginia Sweetspire	*Itea virginica*	X	X	X	
Ferns					
Maidenhair Fern	*Adiantum capillus-veneris*	X	X	X	
Ebony Spleenwort	*Asplenium resiliens*	X	X	X	
Alabama Lipfern	*Cheilanthes alabamensis*	X	X	X	
Powder Cloakfern	*Notholaena dealbata*	X	X	X	
Southern Shield Fern	*Thelypteris ovata* var. *lindheimeri*	X	X	X	

Table 11.2

DEER-RESISTANT PLANTS

Common name	Scientific name	Highly resistant to deer	Deer avoid most of the time	Unpalatable
Annual Sunflower	*Helianthus annuus*			x
Ashe Juniper	*Juniperus ashei*		x	
Bald Cypress	*Taxodium distichum*			x
Beargrass	*Nolina* spp.			x
Black-eyed Susan	*Rudbeckia hirta*			x
Blackfoot Daisy	*Melampodium leucanthum*			x
Cardinal Flower	*Lobelia cardinalis*			x
Cenizo	*Leucophyllum frutescens*			x
Cherry Laurel	*Prunus caroliniana*		x	
Clematis	*Clematis* spp.			x
Columbine	*Aquilegia* spp.			x
Cow-itch Vine	*Cissus trifoliata*			x
Cross-vine	*Bignonia capreolata*			x
Damianita	*Chrysactinia mexicana*	x		
Deciduous Holly	*Ilex decidua*			x
Drummond's Skullcap	*Scutellaria drummondii*			x
Ferns	Almost all except *Pellaea* spp.		x	
Flame-leaf Sumac	*Rhus lanceolata*			x
Fleabane	*Erigeron* spp.			x
Four o'clocks	*Mirabilis* spp.			x
Gayfeather	*Liatris* spp.		x	
Germanders	*Teucrium* spp.			x
Indian Blanket	*Gaillardia pulchella*		x	
Kidneywood	*Eysenhardtia texana*			x
Lantana	*Lantana urticoides*		x	
Larkspur	*Delphinium carolinianum*			x
Lemon Mint	*Monarda citriodora*		x	
Maidenhair Fern	*Adiantum capillus-verneris*		x	
Maximilian Sunflower	*Helianthus maximiliani*			x
Mealy Sage	*Salvia farinacea*		x	
Mexican Hat	*Ratibida columnifera*		x	
Milkweeds	*Asclepias* spp.	x		
Mountain Pink	*Centaurium beyrichii*			x
Penstemons	*Penstemon* spp.			x
Pink Evening Primrose	*Oenothera speciosa*		x	
Pink Wood Sorrel	*Oxalis drummondii*		x	
Prickly Pear Cactus	*Opuntia engelmanni* var. *lindheimeri*			x
Purple Coneflower	*Echinacea purpurea*			x
Queen's Delight	*Stillingia texana*		x	

Common name	Scientific name	Highly resistant to deer	Deer avoid most of the time	Unpalatable
Plateau Liveoak	*Quercus fusiformis*		X	
Red Yucca	*Hesperaloe parviflora*		X	
Eastern Redbud	*Cercis canadensis*			X
Rockcress	*Arabis petiolaris*			X
Shrubby Skullcap	*Scutellaria wrightii*			X
Nightshades	*Solanum* spp.		X	
Shrubby Boneset	*Ageratina havanense*		X	
Slender Greenthread	*Thelesperma filifolium*			X
Snow-on-the-Mountain	*Euphorbia marginata*		X	
Snow-on-the-Prairie	*Euphorbia bicolor*		X	
Texas Mountain-laurel	*Sophora secundiflora*		X	
Texas Persimmon	*Diospyros texana*			X
Texas Sage	*Salvia texana*			X
Verbenas	*Verbena* spp.			X
Yaupon	*Ilex vomitoria*		X	
Yucca	*Yucca rupicola*		X	
Yellow Wood Sorrel	*Oxalis stricta*		X	
Zexmenia	*Wedelia texana*			X

© Paul Montgomery

© Paul Montgomery

Exotics are foreign plants or animals imported and introduced into a new environment. Most gardens in Texas host a number of exotic species of plants. Many have been brought into the United States because of their unusual flowers or fruit, special fragrance, extravagant color, or bizarre appearance. Some may even be horticultural favorites from long ago such as azaleas, roses, and peonies.

The Problem with Exotics

Exotics will sometimes surprise you. While many of them require pesticides, extra water, or cold protection to survive the seasons, some exotics find their new home a dream come true. While not all introductions become invasive, the few that do can become serious problems. Every so often a plant whose origins are continents away will spread unchecked in their new environment, and become "naturalized" in the wild. Slowly and surely, these aliens often out-compete our natives and change the face of the landscape.

Reasons for such unbridled success are manyfold. The most important is the lack of natural controls— no pathogens, no herbivores, or no natural enemies to keep the newcomers down. Because they are foreigners, they have left their native predators and parasites behind and now have little to keep them in check in their new home. Invasive aliens become particularly obnoxious weeds, moving boldly into new habitats and reproducing rapidly.

While a well-planned wildlife garden can have carefully selected exotic plants to serve as accents and supplemental wildlife food sources, using native plants is preferable. The less labor devoted to making ornamental plants survive, the more time to observe the birds and butterflies that frequent your garden. Besides, native plants form the food base for local wildlife species. Their presence in your garden will attract a diversity of animals that do not ordinarily come into residential areas. Gardeners interested in providing habitat for native wildlife should avoid planting exotic plants, and should consider eradicating the ones that have made their way into the landscape.

Common Exotic Plants to Avoid

Its attractive fall foliage and quick growth habit make the exotic Chinese tallow a very popular landscape tree.

CHINESE TALLOW
Sepium sebiferum

The Chinese tallow, an attractive member of the Spurge family, has become the scourge of the Gulf Coast. Spread by birds, this aggressive plant has dramatically altered the landscape of the Upper Texas Coast, out-competing native vegetation at every turn. Like many members of its family, it has milky sap which is poisonous. Originally cultivated in China for the wax from the seed covering which was used for soap, it has now become popular for landscaping because of its fall color and pretty white berries.

CHINESE PRIVET
Ligustrum sinensis

Birds relish the berries of the Chinese privit, another aggressive shrub which is an oriental upstart member of the Olive family. It supplants yaupon and other valuable natives as an understory plant in the wild. Common on the Upper Gulf Coast, this native of southeast Asia is a popular landscape plant grown for its ornamental value.

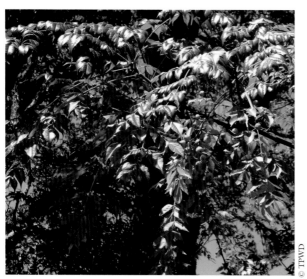

The Chinaberry tree can also be recognized by its distinctive bright yellow fall foliage.

The beautiful blooms of the water-hyacinth belie the danger it poses to rivers, lakes, and streams.

The ubiquitous Chinaberry tree produces pale, fragrant lavender flowers, but is a real pest to native trees.

CHINABERRY TREE
Melia azedarach

A native of Asia, the chinaberry is an introduced ornamental that has escaped cultivation and is growing wild over wide areas of Texas east to Florida. It especially thrives in waste places and along rivers, squeezing out native trees as it spreads. A member of the Mahogany family, its yellow fruit is attractive to birds which disperse the seeds far and wide.

WATER-HYACINTH
Eichhornia crassipes

There is no denying that a carpet of water-hyacinth spread across sluggish streams or lakes is a beautiful sight to behold. It also is a mess to remove, making passage impossible and completely changing the aquatic environment it has overrun.

JAPANESE LIGUSTRUM
Ligustrum japonica

With thick leathery leaves and attractive arrangements of blue berries, the Japanese ligustrum is an ornamental shrub whose spread is aided and abetted by the birds. A member of the Olive family, it has become an all too common invader of Central Texas landscapes, replacing beautiful natives in its wake. Native to China, Korea, and Japan, this aggressive ornamental is commonly planted in the warmer regions of Texas.

PURPLE LOOSESTRIFE
Lythrum salicaria

Purple loosestrife was introduced into North America from Europe at the beginning of the 19th century, and it has progressively spread westward. It aggressively invades wetlands where it displaces native vegetation. While attractive, it takes over moist environments and does not let go. This plant is more of a problem in the northern states, but gardeners should still avoid planting it in Texas.

YELLOW STAR-THISTLE
Centaurea melitensis

Yellow star-thistle is a thorny, noxious weed. This knee-high composite can take over pastures, replacing native forbs and grasses in its path. This aggressive alien is as hard to get rid of as it is unattractive. Many other exotic members of the thistle group, such as nodding thistle and small-flowered thistle, have also become noxious weeds in Texas.

The Japanese honeysuckle vine is a fragrant summer bloomer, but will take over an area if you let it.

JAPANESE HONEYSUCKLE
Lonicera japonica

A clambering, smothering vine, the fragrant exotic honeysuckle can overrun an area once it gets started. Filling the air with a sweet perfume that reminds us of summer and warm weather, it lulls us into thinking that nothing has gone awry. But just try to find another species of plant under a stand of honeysuckle!

Other Problem Plants

Troublesome and aggressive plant species are frequently cultivated in central Texas and often escape into the wild where they replace and out-compete native species. The following species should be avoided as landscape plants and should not be introduced into any Texas habitat, natural or man-made. The notation "(non-native)" indicates a variety or species which is not native to Texas. There are other varieties or specific species of these groups of plants that are native to the state, which you may include in a Wildscape without harm.

TREES AND SHRUBS

Tree-of-heaven
  Ailanthus altissima
Mimosa tree
  Albizia julibrissin
Paper mulberry
  Broussonetia papyrifera
Chinese loquat
  Eriobotrya japonica
Common fig
  Ficus carica
Chinese parasol-tree
  Firmiana simplex
Golden rain-tree
  Koelreuteria paniculata
Lantana (non-native)
  Lantana spp. (non-native varieties)
Wax-leaf ligustrum
  Ligustrum quihoui
White mulberry
  Morus alba
Heavenly bamboo
  Nandina domestica

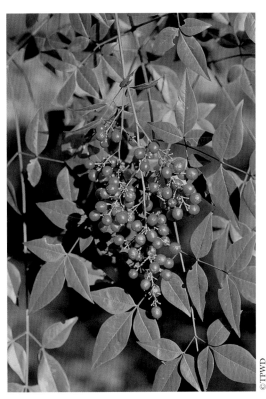

The bright red berries of a nandina provide much needed color in winter, but the plant can be rather aggressive when it escapes cultivation.

Oleander
  Nerium oleander
Red-tip photinia
  Photinia serratifolia
White poplar
  Populus alba
Kudzu
  Pueraria montana var. *lobata*
Firethorn
  Pyracantha spp.
Salt cedar
  Tamarix spp.
Siberian elm
  Ulmus pumila
Periwinkle
  Vinca major
Lilac chaste-tree
  Vitex agnus-castus

HERBACEOUS PLANTS
Many-flowered thistle
  Carduus tenuiflorus
Nodding thistle
  Carduus nutans
Distaff thistle
  Carthamus lanatus
Malta star-thistle
  Centaurea melitensis
Chicory
  Cichorium intybus
Tickseed, tick-clover
  Desmodium spp.
Bush-clover
  Lespedeza spp. (non-native varieties)
Birdsfoot trefoil
  Lotus corniculatus
Common horehound
  Marrubium vulgare
Sweet clover
  Melilotus albus
Sour clover
  Melilotus indicus
Yellow sweet clover
  Melilotus offinalis
Childing pink
  Petrorhagia prolifer

Wild mustard
  Rapistrum rugosum
Castor-bean
  Ricinus communis
Tumbleweed
  Salsola kali
Milk thistle
  Silybum marianum
Sow thistle
  Sonchus asper
Beggar's ticks
  Torilis arvensis
Goats's beard
  Tragopogon dubius
Low hop-clover
  Trifolium campestre
White clover
  Trifolium repens
Pink clover
  Trifolium pratense
Brazilian vervain
  Verbena brasiliensis
Persian speedwell
  Veronica persica

GRASSES
Giant reed
  Arundo donax
KR Bluestem
  Bothriochloa ischaemum

Johnsongrass is used extensively in agriculture, but will also invade native prairies, meadows, and even urban landscapes.

Japanese honeysuckle (Lonicera japonica).

Rip-gut brome
Bromus diandrus
Rescuegrass
Bromus catharticus
Bufflegrass
Pennisetum ciliare var. *ciliare*
Bermudagrass
Cynodon dactylon
Kleberg bluestem
Dichanthium annulatum
Angleton bluestem
Dichanthium aristatum
Silky bluestem
Dichanthium sericeum

Goosegrass
Eleusine indica
Mediterranean lovegrass
Eragrostis barrelieri
Tall fescue
Lolium arundinaceum
Meadow fescue
Lolium pratense
Kleingrass
Panicum coloratum
Bahia grass
Paspalum notatum
Johnsongrass
Sorghum halepense
Guineagrass
Urochloa maxima

AQUATIC PLANTS
Elephant ears
Colocasia spp.
Water hyacinth
Eichhornia crassipes
Hydrilla
Hydrilla verticillata
Yellow flag
Iris pseudacorus
Purple loosestrife
Lythrum salicaria
Milfoil
Myriophyllum spp. (non-native)

ACHENE: A small, dry, one-seeded fruit with no seams, as in a sunflower.

ACID SOIL: Soils which have a low pH; deficient in lime.

ALKALINE SOIL: Soils rich lime; having a high pH.

ALTERNATE: Any leaf arrangement along the stem that is not opposite or whorled. Only one leaf arising from the node.

ANGIOSPERM: Plants that produce seeds enclosed in a fleshy, papery, or woody fruit; a flowering plant.

ANNUAL: A plant that germinates from seed, flowers, sets seed, and dies in the same year.

ANTENNA (plural antennae): Paired structures on the head of the butterfly, probably used for smelling, touching, and orientation. In butterflies the antennae are clubbed or barely thickened. In skippers they are hooked at the end like a shepherd's crook. Moths can have plumed antennae.

ANTHER: The pollen-bearing part of the stamen.

APODIFORMES: The avian order that includes swifts and hummingbirds. The name refers to the characteristic of both swifts and hummingbirds as having extremely weak legs and feet suitable for perching or clinging, but not for walking.

APOSEMATISM: Vivid coloration or striking pattern, often in reds, yellows, oranges, and black, that identifies an animal as having distasteful or unpleasant properties. Warning coloration.

AQUATIC: Primarily inhabiting water.

ARID: Areas where annual precipitation is less than the potential evaporation and transpiration. An area which typically has very little soil moisture.

AROMATIC: Fragrant, spicy or pungent in smell. Usually refers to a scent given off when you crush the leaves.

ARROYO: A gully generally found along valley floors in an arid or semi-arid region. The gully has steep walls cut into fine-grained sediments. The floor is flat and is generally sandy. In the United States, arroyos are typically found in the Southwest.

ASCENDING: Rising or curving obliquely in an upward direction.

AXIL: The angle formed between the leaf and the stem to which it is attached.

BARBS: The individual subunits of a feather, which extend diagonally outward in pairs from the central shaft. Barbs contain the pigments which are responsible for the feather's color.

BATESIAN MIMICRY: Resemblance of a palatable species to one that is unpalatable or has effective defenses. This may trick a predator into passing up an otherwise tasty prey item.

BENEFICIAL INSECTS: Insects that feed on other insects that are destructive to plants.

BIENNIAL: A plant that completes its life cycle in two years.

BOG: A plant community in acidic, wet areas. Decomposition rates are very slow, which favors the development of peat.

BRACT: A reduced or modified leaf found just underneath the flower cluster. Looks like a petal but is not.

BULB: Underground storage organ filled with resources formed during the previous growing season to nurture the next season's blooms.

BULB SCALES: The fleshy, overlapping segments on the bulbs of lilies.

CALCAREOUS: Consisting of a large portion of calcium carbonate. Used when referring to soils.

CALICHE: A white to cream-colored carbonate soil made from decomposed limestone.

CALYX: Refers collectively to the outer whorl of flower parts, usually green. The sum of the sepals.

CAMPANULATE: Shaped like a bell. Refers to flower shape.

CANEBRAKE: A thicket of cane.

CAPSULE: A dry fruit that consists of two or more parts that split open.

CARPEL: Also called pistil, the female part of the flower which bears the ovules.

CATKIN: A scaly spike of reduced flowers.

CHAPARRAL: An area of vegetation characterized by plants having leaves which are evergreen, hard, thick, leathery, and usually small.

CHENIER: A beach or sandy ridge that is built on a marsh area. Formed by the working of waves on river sediment in the Gulf Coast of Texas.

CHITIN: The tough material that makes up a major part of an insect's inner cuticle or procuticle. The procuticle is part of the insect's outer skeleton (exoskeleton).

CIENEGA: A spring-fed wetland. In Texas, used for such areas in the Southwest portions of the state.

CLUTCH: In egg-laying animals, a complete set of eggs laid and incubated at one time.

COMPLETE METAMORPHOSIS: Striking changes between larva and adult, with an intervening pupal stage, as in insects.

COMPOST: The rotting down of organic material for use as humus.

COMPOUND LEAF: A leaf composed of smaller, distinct, bladelike parts called leaflets.

CONIFEROUS: Applies to trees or shrubs that are mostly evergreen and generally bear seeds in cones.

CONNATE: United at the base. Usually refers to the joining of the bottom part of blades of opposite leaves. Fusion of like parts.

CONTOUR FEATHERS: The body feathers in general, not including the more specialized types of feathers such as down.

CORDATE: Heart-shaped, especially when referring to a leaf.

COROLLA: The inner, colored whorl of flower parts. Refers to all the petals collectively.

CREPUSCULAR: Active during the twilight hours of dawn and dusk.

CULTIVARS: Plant varieties found only under cultivation.

DECIDUOUS: Applies to trees that shed their leaves seasonally.

DELTOID: Triangular in shape, especially when referring to a leaf.

DESERT: An area in which the amount of precipitation is exceeded by the amount of evaporation for most of the time. Plants and animals that occupy deserts have adapted to long periods of drought or lack of free water.

DIAPAUSE: A state of arrested growth, development, and behavior that occurs at a particular stage in an insect's life cycle.

DISK FLOWER: A small tubular flower that is found on the central disk of a flower in the Sunflower family (Compositae).

DISPLAY: Behavior patterns that have evolved to provide a means for one organism to communicate with another. Displays are often stereotypic and exaggerated. Territoriality or mate suitability are often the message.

DIURNAL: Active during the daylight hours, as opposed to nocturnal.

DRUPE: A fleshy fruit with one stonelike seed in the center, as in a plum or a peach.

ECOSYSTEMS: An interdependent community of organisms and the environment in which they live.

EDGE: The transitional zone where two habitats meet.

ELLIPTIC: Narrowly oval in shape, most often twice as long as wide, when talking about leaf shape.

ENDEMIC: Referring to a species of animal or plant which is native to and restricted to a particular region.

ENTIRE: When speaking about the margin of a leaf, completely smooth and unbroken; no teeth.

ESTUARY: A coastal area in which salt water from the sea and fresh water from inland rivers mix. Estuaries are often subject to tidal action, and the ebb and flood currents avoid one another, forming separate channels.

EXOSKELETON: A skeleton external to the remainder of the body, with the muscles attaching to its inner surface, as in an insect.

EXOTIC: A plant that has been introduced into an area; a non-native.

FASCICLE: A compact cluster or bundle, as of pine needles.

FILAMENT: In flowers, the stalklike structure that bears the anther in a stamen.

FILIFORM: Shaped like thin threads.

FLEDGLING PERIOD: The period between the first flight and gaining independence.

FOLLICLE: In plants, a type of fruit that is dry, opens automatically and along one line.

FOREST: A vegetated area in which the tree crowns touch, and so form a continuous canopy.

GENERALIST: A species with broad foraging or habitat requirements. Such an animal would not be dependent on a single environmental resource, such as only one or two plant species. Most hummingbirds are generalists.

GERMINATION: The beginning of growth of a seed, usually after a period of dormancy.

GLABROUS: Smooth and lacking hairs.

GLAND: A structure on or beneath a surface which secretes a substance.

GLOBOSE: Round or spherical in shape.

GORGET: The brightly colored, iridescent throat patch of a hummingbird which shines brightly when the light hits it at the proper angle.

GYMNOSPERM: Plants that produce seeds held in woody or fleshy cones.

HABITAT: The physical characteristics of a specific environment.

HALOPHYTIC: A plant that is adapted to salty environments.

HAWKING: The act of capturing insects while in flight.

HEAD: In plants, a dense flower cluster that rises from a common point on a stem.

HERBACEOUS: Herblike. Leafy and green, definitely nonwoody.

HOLOMETABOLOUS: Having complete metamorphosis. Passing through egg, larval, pupal, and adult stages. Butterflies are holometabolous.

HUMUS: Partially decomposed organic matter.

IMAGO: The terminal instar, or the adult stage, of an insect.

INCISED: Deeply cut.

INCUBATION PERIOD: In birds, the period between the laying of eggs and hatching, when one or both parents actively sit on the nest to warm the eggs.

INFLORESCENCE: The flower cluster or flower head of a plant consisting of many smaller florets. infructescence: The inflorescence in its fruiting stage.

INNATE: Inherited, such as instinctive patterns of behavior.

INSTAR: The stage of an insect's development between molts, the first being between hatching and the first larval molt.

INVASIVE PLANTS: Plants that spread aggressively into areas where other plants are growing.

IRIDESCENCE: A spectral color formed by selective interference and reflection of specific wavelengths of light, as in hummingbird feathers.

LACINIATE: Cut into slender lobes or segments.

LATERAL: On the side of something.

LEACHING: The process of removing material from a substrate with percolating liquid (liquid passing through a porous substance).

LEAF LITTER: A layer of fallen and decaying leaves.

LEGUME: A plant in the pea family that produces a dry pod opening along two lines.

LEPIDOPTERA: The order to which butterflies and moths belong. Second in size only to Coleoptera, to which the beetles belong.

LEPIDOPTERIST: A person who studies butterflies and moths.

LINEAR: Narrow and long.

LOAM: A soil composed of a balanced mixture of silt, sand, and clay.

LYRATE: Having or suggesting the shape of a lyre.

MANGROVE FOREST: A forest located in a swamp of saline or brackish (mixture of both fresh and saline) water. Typically, the forest has a tangle of roots which project above the surface of the water. Mangrove forests can reach over ninety feet tall, but in Texas they are short and not common.

MARGIN: The outer edge of a leaf.

MARINE: Having to do with the sea.

MARSH: An ecosystem of more or less continuously waterlogged soil dominated by emersed herbaceous plants, but without a surface accumulation of peat.

MESA: A flat-topped hill that is similar in form to but smaller than a plateau. Both are smaller than a butte, which is a flat-topped hill where the diameter of the caprock is less than the height of the land from above the surrounding country.

MIMICRY: The resemblance of one organism to another or to an object in its surroundings for concealment and protection against predators.

MOBBING: An aggressive behavior of small birds often associated with the presence of a predator. Birds will fly at, peck, and harass the predator until it leaves the area.

MONTANE FOREST: A forested area at high elevations as on a mountain. It is comprised of vegetation that is different from vegetation at the same latitude but lower altitude. Trees are smaller and species diversity is generally reduced.

MORPHOLOGY: The form and structure of any object, especially organisms, without the consideration of function.

MUCRONATE: A leaf having a small, short projection at the tip.

MUDFLAT: An area along the coast where fine grained silt or sediment and clay accumulates. It is an early state in the development of a saltmarsh or mangrove forest.

MUELLERIAN MIMICRY: The similarity in appearance of one species to another, where both are unpalatable.

MULCH: A protective layer of organic material placed around the plant to retain soil moisture and restrict weed growth. Leaves, straw, or peat help prevent evaporation and freezing of the roots.

NATIVE PLANTS: Plants that grow naturally in an area without human influence or interference.

NATURALIZED PLANTS: Non-native or introduced plants adapted sufficiently enough to an area to be able to reproduce in the wild.

NECTAR GUIDE: A streak on a flower that guides the pollinating agent such as a bee, moth, butterfly, or hummingbird to the nectar source. It may also work to guide the sharp bill of the hummingbird away from the delicate ovary of the flowering plant. Some nectar guides are invisible to humans, but are plainly evident to insects sensitive to ultraviolet light.

NECTARIVOROUS: Organisms adapted for foraging on nectar.

NEMATODES: Minute, unsegmented soil-inhabiting worms of the phylum Nematoda.

NERVE: In a leaf blade, the vein, groove, or rib on the upper or lower surface.

NESTING PERIOD: The period between hatching and initial flight in birds.

NICHE: The role that a species occupies in nature; that is, its precise habitat plus its behavior in that habitat. (Its profession, as opposed to its address.)

NOCTURNAL: Active primarily at night. Compare to diurnal and crepuscular.

NODE: The point on a stem from which the leaves arise. Looks like a swollen bump along the stem.

NUPTIAL PLUMAGE: Plumage associated with the breeding season. Also called alternate plumage.

OBLONG: Much longer than broad in shape, usually with parallel sides.

OLD GROWTH: A mature ecosystem characterized by the presence of old woody plants and the wildlife and smaller plants associated with them.

OMMATIDIUM (PLURAL OMMATIDIA): A functional unit of the compound eye, expressed externally as a facet.

OPPOSITE LEAVES: Paired leaf arrangement, with one leaf on either side of the stem at the node.

ORBICULAR: More or less round in shape, as in a leaf.

ORNITHOPHILOUS: Refers to a special class of bird-pollinated plants with special floral adaptations such as distinctive coloration, high nectar production, thick-skinned tubular blossoms and general lack of fragrance, which are attractive to birds. In the Western Hemisphere, hummingbirds are the principal beneficiaries of these special adaptations.

OUTCROP: That part of a geologic formation, like a limestone ledge, that projects out from the surrounding soil.

OVARY: The ovule-bearing lower part of a pistil that ripens into fruit.

OVULE: In flowers, the minute structure that, after fertilization, becomes the seed.

PALPUS (PLURAL PALPI): In insects, a paired, segmented appendage arising on the maxilla or labium (mouth area) and serving sensory functions associated with taking in food.

PANICLE: A branched cluster of flowers in which the branches are racemes.

PARASITE: A plant or animal that derives its nourishment from another living plant or animal (host) and that completes its development on or in another host. The parasite does not normally kill its host.

PARASITOID: An insect that lives its immature stages in or on another insect, which it kills after completing its own feeding.

PEAT: An accumulation of unconsolidated partially decomposed plant material in a more or less waterlogged area. See marsh.

PEDICEL: The supporting stalk of a single flower in a flower cluster.

PEDUNCLE: A general term for the stem of a single flower or a group of flowers.

PELTATE: A leaf having its stem attached to the center of the lower surface of the blade as in Pennywort.

PENDULOUS: Hanging or drooping.

PERENNIAL: A plant of indefinite life span, flowering and setting seed each year.

PERFECT: In plants, flowers that have both male and female sex organs present and functioning.

PETIOLE: The stalk of a leaf.

PH: A measure of the acidity or alkalinity of a medium. High pH is basic or alkaline, low pH is acidic.

PHEROMONE: An external chemical messenger that passes between individuals of the same species and controls intraspecific interactions, i.e. attracting mates, recognizing mate, responding to mating signals, etc.

PINNATE: A compound leaf with the leaflets symmetrically arranged on both sides of a common stem.

PISTIL: Includes the stigma, style and ovary of the flower. It bears the ovules, like carpel.

PLAYA: A nearly level area at the bottom of an undrained basin that frequently floods, affording excellent habitat for breeding ducks and shore birds.

PLUMOSE: Featherlike in appearance.

POD: A dry fruit that opens along seams like a legume.

POLLEN: Collectively, the mass of microspores or pollen grains produced by the male parts (anthers) of flowering plants or male cones of gymnosperms (like pine trees).

POLLINATION: The transfer of pollen from the anther to the stigma of the same flower or of another flower, by wind, insects, or hummingbirds.

PRAIRIE: An area of vegetation in North America dominated by drought-resistant grasses. Prairies are characterized by the height of their dominant grasses, i.e. shortgrass, midgrass, and tallgrass.

PRICKLE: A sharp outgrowth of the bark or epidermis of a plant. Compare to spine and thorn.

PROBOSCIS: A slender, strawlike tube, used by the butterfly to drink nectar and other fluids. When not feeding, it is kept tightly coiled underneath the insect's head. The length varies from species to species.

PROCUMBENT: In plants, trailing on the ground but not rooting.

PROSTRATE: Lying flat on the ground. Often used when referring to the habits or character of plants.

PUBESCENT: Covered with hairs.

RACEME: A spikelike floral arrangement consisting of a central axis stem bearing a number of flowers on pedicels of equal length. The basal flower opens slightly earlier than its neighbors. Two good examples of racemous flowers are the blue larkspur (*Delphinium carolinianum*) and pale lobelia (*Lobelia appendiculata*).

RAY FLOWER: In the composite flower of the Sunflower family, the outer, nonfertile straplike flowers surrounding the fertile disk flowers.

RENIFORM: Shaped like a kidney, especially when referring to a leaf, as in Texas redbud.

RETICULATE: Having a netlike pattern, as on the undersurface of a leaf.

RHIZOME: A horizontal underground stem that develops roots and sends up leaves and flowering stems.

RIPARIAN: Pertaining to a riverbank.

ROOST: A place to rest or sleep, especially in birds.

SAMARA: A winged fruit, as in a maple tree or an ash.

SAVANNAH: An extensive area dominated by grasses and accompanied by tall bushes or trees. Characterized as "open," a grassland with a scattering of tress and shrubs.

SCAPE: A flower stalk rising up from the ground and bearing one or more flowers, but no leaves, as in a rainlily.

SECONDARY SUCCESSION: The type of vegetation that appears after an environmental disturbance, such as burning.

SEPAL: A green, leaflike segment of the calyx.

SERRATE: A toothed margin of a leaf with the teeth pointing forward.

SESSILE: A condition where the leaf blade attaches directly to the stem without a petiole or stalk.

SEXUAL DIMORPHISM: Refers to species in which the two sexes differ markedly as adults, either in size, color, or behavior.

SILIQUE: The fruit of many members of the Mustard family. A capsule which peels away from a central dividing membrane.

SIMPLE: An undivided, nonbranched leaf which is not compound.

SINUATE: Deeply or strongly wavy along the leaf margin.

SLOUGH: An inlet from a river, backwater, creek in a marsh, or tidal flat.

SNAG: Standing dead tree.

SPECIALIST: A species with narrow foraging or habitat adaptations. A specialist, unlike a generalist, will exploit a single resource.

SPINE: A sharp-pointed, rigid structure which is really a highly modified leaf. Compare to prickle and thorn.

SPIRACLE: An external opening of the tracheal system that takes in air. Insects, such as butterflies, breathe through these tiny holes which are located in a row along each side of the thorax and abdomen.

STAMEN: The part of the flower that produces pollen, including the anthers and filaments. The male component of the flower.

STELLATE: Having radiating arms or shaped like a star.

STIGMA: The surface of the female flower part or pistil that receives the pollen.

STIPULES: Pairs of very reduced leaflike appendages that are found at the base of the petiole of a leaf.

STRIATE: Having very fine grooves, ridges or lines along the axis.

SUCCESSION: The process of change by which a stable, natural plant community is reached, progressing from initial disturbance to climax.

SUCCULENT: Very fleshy, juicy, and soft, as in a cactus pad.

SWALE: A low-lying, wet stretch of land.

SWAMP: A wet area that is more or less permanently covered in water, not drying out in the summer. A seasonally flooded bottomland with more woody plants than a marsh.

TAPROOT: A large, central root.

TAXONOMY: The practice of classifying organisms and arranging them in an ordered system that reflects natural relationships.

TENDRIL: A coiling or twining organ by which the plant climbs, seen often in vines.

TEPALS: Collectively, the petals and the sepals, especially when they cannot be differentiated.

TERRESTRIAL: Primarily inhabiting land. Compare with aquatic.

TERRITORIALITY: The advertisement and aggressive behavior associated with establishing and defending a territory, especially during the breeding season.

TERRITORY: An area having resources that are controlled or defended by an animal against others of its species. For example, hummingbird territories usually contain important food sources which are vigorously defended by the territory holder.

THERMOREGULATION: Temperature regulation. Many insects and reptiles are cold-blooded, or ectothermic, organisms. On cool days, these animals can absorb heat from the sun several ways, including basking or shivering. On warmer or hot days, warm-blooded, or endothermic organisms avoid or release heat by hiding in shade, panting, and sweating.

THORAX: The central segment of an insect's body, bearing the legs and wings.

THORN: A modified branch that is sharp-pointed. Compare to spine and prickle.

THORN FOREST, THORN SCRUB, THORN WOODLAND: An area of vegetation that is dominated by thorny shrubs and bushy trees, perhaps with a few taller trees. Ground plants generally do not include grasses, which reflects the more arid nature of thorn scrub habitat. Common in south Texas.

THROAT: In a flower, the central opening of the flower in a corolla composed of fused petals.

TIDAL FLAT: In coastal areas, a sand flat, mud flat, or marsh developed in tidal areas, estuaries, or protected bays of some lagoons.

TORPOR: A sleeplike state of reduced body temperature and metabolism, often entered into during the night or during cold periods of the year. An excellent energy conserving strategy. Used by poorwills and hummingbirds, for example.

TRACHEA: A delicate system of air tubes. Insects, such as butterflies, do not have lungs as we do, so the tracheal system supplies oxygen to every cell.

TROCHILIDAE: The family of birds to which hummingbirds belong.

TUBER: A short, thickened underground stem which bears many buds.

UMBEL: A flat-topped or convex flower cluster in which the pedicels arise from a common point, as in many flowers of the parsley family.

UNDULATE: Wavy, often used when speaking about a leaf margin.

UNIFOLIOLATE: Having only one leaf or leaflet.

VEIN (OF A WING): In insects, a hardened rod supporting the wing membrane (collectively called venation).

VESICLE: A cavity or bladder.

WETLANDS: Collectively, an area that is covered in water permanently or seasonally. A general term that includes swamps, bogs, fens, marshes, lakes, ponds, rivers, and estuarine habitats.

WHORL: A circular arrangement of three or more petals or leaves at one node (joint).

WING: In plants, a ribbonlike membrane bordering a stem or around seeds.

WOODLAND: An area in which the widely spaced, mature tree crowns do not necessarily touch, giving a more or less open appearance. Under the trees, grasses, heath, and scrub communities often develop, giving the area a parklike appearance.

XERIC: Referring to arid or desert conditions. Not needing much water for survival. Compare to mesic and hydric.

XERISCAPE: To landscape with plants that require little or no supplemental water.

Bibliography and Reading List

Plant Field Guides and Information

Ajilvsgi, G. 1979. *Wildflowers of the Big Thicket, East Texas, and Western Louisiana*. College Station, Texas: Texas A&M University Press.

——. 1984. *Wildflowers of Texas*. Bryan, Texas: Shearer Publishing Inc.

Amos, C., and F. Gehlbach, eds. 1988. *Edwards Plateau Vegetation: Plant Ecological studies in Central Texas*. Waco, Texas: Baylor University Press.

Brown, C. A. 1972. *Wildflowers of Louisiana and Adjoining States*. Baton Rouge, Louisiana: Louisiana State University Press.

Cannatella, M. 1985. *Plants of the Texas Shore: A Beachcombers Guide*. College Station, Texas: Texas A&M University Press.

Correll, D., and M. Johnston. 1979. *Manual of the Vascular Plants of Texas*. Richardson, Texas: University of Texas.

Cox, P., and P. Leslie. 1988. *Texas Trees; A Friendly Guide*. San Antonio, Texas: Corona Press.

Duncan, W. H., and M. B. Duncan. 1987. *The Smithsonian Guide to Seaside Plants of the Gulf and Atlantic Coasts*. Washington, D.C.: Smithsonian Institution Press.

Enquist, M. 1987. *Wildflowers of the Texas Hill Country*. Austin, Texas: Lone Star Botanical.

Everitt, J. H., and D. L. Drawe. 1993. *Trees, Shrubs, and Cacti of South Texas*. Lubbock, Texas: Texas Tech University Press.

Gould, F. 1975. *The Grasses of Texas*. College Station, Texas: Texas A&M University Press.

Great Plains Flora Association. 1977. *Atlas of the Flora of the Great Plains*. Ames, Iowa: Iowa State University Press.

Ham, H. 1984. *South Texas Wildflowers*. Kingsville, Texas: The Conner Museum, Texas A&I University.

Hatch, S. L., and J. Pluhar. 1995. *Texas Range Plants*. College Station, Texas: Texas A&M University Press.

Jones, F. 1975. *Flora of the Texas Coastal Bend*. Corpus Christi, Texas: Mission Press.

Kirkpatrick, Z. M. 1992. *Wildflowers of the Western Plains*. Austin, Texas: University of Texas Press.

Lonard, R. I., and F. W. Judd. 1981. *The Terrestrial Flora of South Padre Island, Texas*. Misc. Paper #6. Austin, Texas: Texas Memorial Museum, University of Texas at Austin.

Lonard, R. I., J. H. Everitt, and F. W. Judd. 1991. *Woody Plants of the Lower Rio Grande Valley Texas*. Misc. Paper #7. Austin, Texas: Texas Memorial Museum, University of Texas at Austin.

Loughmiller, C., and L. Loughmiller. 1984. *Texas Wildflowers: A Field Guide*. Austin, Texas. University of Texas Press.

Lynch, Brother D. 1981. *Native and Naturalized Woody Plants of Austin and The Hill Country*. Austin, Texas: Saint Edward's University.

Mahler, W. F. 1988. *Shinner's Manual of the North Central Texas Flora*. Fort Worth, Texas: Botanical Research Institute of Texas.

Nixon, E. 1985. *Trees, Shrubs, and Woody Vines of East Texas*. Nacogdoches, Texas: Bruce Lyndon Cunningham Productions.

Powell, M. A. 1988. *Trees and Shrubs of Trans-Pecos Texas Including Big Bend and Guadalupe Mountains National Park*. Big Bend National Park, Texas: Big Bend Natural History Association, Incorporated.

Richardson, A. 1990. *Plants of Southernmost Texas*. Brownsville, Texas: University of Texas at Brownsville.

Rose, F., and R. Strandtmann. 1986. *Wildflowers of the Llano Estacado*. Dallas, Texas: Taylor Publishing Company.

Simpson, B. J. 1989. *A Field Guide to Texas Trees*. Austin, Texas: Texas Monthly Press.

Tveten, J., and G. Tveten. 1993. *Wildflowers of Houston.* Houston, Texas: Rice University Press.

Vines, R. A. 1960. *Trees, Shrubs, and Woody Vines of the Southwest.* Austin, Texas: University of Texas Press.

———. 1982. *Trees of North Texas.* Austin, Texas: University of Texas Press.

Warnock, B.H. 1970. *Wildflowers of the Big Bend Country, Texas.* Alpine, Texas: Sul Ross University Press.

———. 1974. *Wildflowers of the Guadalupe Mountains and the Sand Dune Country, Texas.* Alpine, Texas: Sul Ross University Press.

———. 1977. *Wildflowers of the Davis Mountains and the Marathon Basin, Texas.* Alpine, Texas: Sul Ross University Press.

Wildlife Field Guides and Information

Davis, W. B., and D. J. Schmidly. 1994. *The Mammals of Texas.* Austin, Texas: University of Texas Press.

Garrett, J. M., and D. G. Barker. 1987. *A Field Guide to Reptiles and Amphibians of Texas.* Houston, Texas: Gulf Publishing Company.

Martin, A. C., H. S. Zim, and A. L. Nelson. 1951. *American Wildlife and Plants—A Guide to Wildlife Food Habits.* New York: Dover Publications.

National Geographic Society. 1987. *Field Guide to the Birds of North America, Second Edition.* Washington, D. C.: National Geographic Society.

Rappole, J. H., and G. W. Blacklock. 1985. *Birds of the Coastal Bend: Abundance and Distribution.* College Station: Texas A&M University Press.

Stokes, D., and L. Stokes. 1989. *The Hummingbird Book.* Boston, Massachusetts: Little, Brown, and Company.

Tennant, A. 1985. *A Field Guide to Texas Snakes.* Houston, Texas: Gulf Publishing Company.

Toops, C. 1992. *Hummingbirds: Jewels in Flight.* Stillwater, Minnesota: Voyageur Press, Incorporated.

Tveten, J. L. 1993. *The Birds of Texas.* Fredericksburg, Texas: Shearer Publishing.

Wildlife Landscaping/Gardening in Texas

Garrett, J. H. 1996. *Plants for Texas.* Austin, Texas: University of Texas Press.

Wasowski, S., and A. Wasowski. 1989. *Native Texas Plants: Landscaping Region by Region.* Austin, Texas: Texas Monthly Press.

———. 1997. *Native Texas Gardens.* Austin, Texas: Texas Monthly Press.

Wildlife Landscaping/Gardening (Not Region Specific)

Ajilvsgi, G. 1991. *Butterfly Gardening for the South.* Dallas, Texas: Taylor Publishing Company.

Ellis, B. 1997. *Attracting Birds and Butterflies: How to Plan and Plant a Backyard Habitat.* Boston, Massachusetts: Houghton Mifflin Company.

Garrett, J. H. 1995. *The Dirt Doctor's Guide to Organic Gardening.* Austin, Texas: University of Texas Press.

Peterson, R. T. et al. 1974. *Gardening with Wildlife.* Washington, D.C.: National Wildlife Federation.

Pope, T., N. Oldenwald, and C. Fryling. 1993. *Attracting Birds to Southern Gardens.* Dallas: Taylor Publishing Company.

Tufts, C. 1988. *The Backyard Naturalist.* Washington, D. C.: National Wildlife Federation.

Wilson, J. 1991. *Landscaping with Wildflowers.* Boston: Houghton Mifflin Company.

Wildlife and Habitat Management

Fisher, C. D. 1984. Texas birds: diversity and preservation. In: *Protection of Texas Natural Diversity: An Introduction for Natural Resource Planners and Managers.* (eds.) E. G. Carls and J. Neal. College Station, Texas: Texas A&M University Press.

Ecology of Texas

Flores, D. L. 1990. *Caprock Canyonlands: Journeys into the Heart of the Southern Plains.* Austin, Texas: University of Texas Press.

Gould, F., G. O. Hoffman, and C. A. Rechenthin. 1960. *Vegetational Areas of Texas.* College Station, Texas: Texas Agricultural Experiment Station L-492.

Texas General Land Office. 1980. "The Natural Heritage of Texas." Austin, Texas: Nature Conservancy.

Wauer, R. H. 1980. *Naturalist's Big Bend.* College Station, Texas: Texas A&M University Press.

Weaver, J. E. 1954. *North American Prairie.* Lincoln, Nebraska: Johnsen Publishing Company.

Winckler, S. 1982. Texas Diversity: From the Piney Woods to the Trans-Pecos. In: *The Nature Conservancy News:* 32(5).

Notes